DUNDEE

University Library

Date of Return - Subject to Recall

REPRESENTATIVE DEMOCRACY AND ITS LIMITS

Paul Hirst

Polity Press

95·131340 (1)

First published 1990 by Polity Press
in association with Basil Blackwell

Editorial office:
Polity Press
65 Bridge Street, Cambridge CB2 1UR, UK

Marketing and production:
Basil Blackwell Ltd
108 Cowley Road, Oxford OX4 1JF, UK

ISBN 0 7456 0678 4

British Library Cataloguing in Publication Data
A CIP catalogue record for this book is
available from the British Library.

Typeset in 10 on 12 pt Times
by Wearside Tradespools, Fulwell, Sunderland
Printed in Great Britain by TJ Press, Padstow

Contents

1

Introduction

Western representative democracy is now secure in a way it has never been for the better part of this century. In the 1930s the European democracies were threatened by fascist and Stalinist parties within and states without. At the risk of extinction as an institution, democracy was also radically and brutally challenged as a body of ideas. At the core of fascism and Marxism-Leninism as political doctrines was a root and branch critique of representative democracy. Representative democracy was claimed to be a partial and inadequate form of democracy tied to 'bourgeois liberalism' and destined to be extinguished by the new political movements which claimed to represent the future. The defeat of the Axis powers in 1945 did not end the institutional threat to democracy, for Stalinist communism and its successor regimes in the Soviet Union extinguished democracy in Eastern Europe after 1945 and suppressed movements for democratization whenever they reasserted themselves into the 1980s. Nor did the intellectual threat entirely cease, despite the fact that fascist and Marxist-Leninist ideas had lost all credence in the West. Central to the student movements of the 1960s was a rejection of representative democracy in favour of participatory and direct democracy.

In the 1980s Western representative democracy is not only unchallenged but is emulated by the very movements that previously sought its extinction. There are no credible forces seeking to overthrow Western polities. The left in Western Europe, including the major communist parties, is almost exclusively parliamentary-democratic, accepting multi-party democracy as a point of principle. In Eastern Europe, Poland and Hungary are cautiously moving toward multi-party pluralism. The Soviet Union has accepted the need for contested elections and a genuinely functioning representative assembly. Even the brutal repression of the movement for democratization in China has served to prove two things: one, the commitment of the students to Western democratic ideas, symbolized by their building a Statue of Liberty in Tiananmen Square; the other, the reinforcement in world opinion of the rightness of the students' struggle for democracy.

All this is doubtless obvious to any half-informed observer, but some of the implications are less obvious. The left has embraced democracy. It has accepted representative government, multi-party elections and mass electorates. Yet in doing so it faces two major problems. The first is that forms of representative democracy deliver very low levels of governmental accountability and public influence on decision-making. Compared to Stalinism and fascism the chance to vote out the government is an inestimable benefit. But remove that threat and modern mass democracy fails badly, by the standards set by its own proponents. The left is accepting and endorsing a failing system of democratic accountability. The left is also accepting a process of political competition in which parties of the left can win at best periodically and in which, when they do win, the scope for large-scale social and political change by parliamentary means is severely restricted.[1]

In embracing representative democracy the left has been forced to abandon the aim of building a socialist society – bringing the means of production, distribution and exchange into public ownership and control. The left as a whole in the democratic West has taken the better part of a century to discover that Bernstein was right. How has it responded to this discovery? In the case of large sections of the socialist intelligentsia, it has done so largely by centring on the issue of democratization. The advocacy of democracy has a double function: on the one hand, democratization of the state and the wider society provides an alternative left objective and strategy to the traditional socialist aim of socializing the means of production; on the other hand, the proposed forms of extension of democracy are a counter to the major defects of representative democracy which limit the scope for left political initiative. The intellectual left in Europe and the United States has adopted democratization as the core of its political advocacy. This is more than fashion or happenstance; it is a response to the conjuncture in which representative democracy has become unchallengeable and unsurpassable.

The problem is, therefore, how to propose further democratization without a root and branch critique of representative democracy. How, moreover, to face the fact of the exhaustion of the radical critiques of representative democracy, like Marxism. The answer of the democratic left is to raid the storehouse of Western liberalism and democratic theory. Almost without exception the intellectual left have adopted non-Marxist and non-traditional socialist ideas to advance the cause of democratization. They have had to. Marxism offers no viable political theory. The turning from Marxism is no mere 'revisionist' fashion, as the surviving fundamentalist Marxists seem to think, rather it is a precondition of relevant and politically credible argument in a representative-democratic polity.

How have the new democratic left responded to the problem of advocating radical democratization without advocating the destruction of the existing representative democratic system? First, let us note the exceptions. Some post-industrial utopian and green thinkers do advocate small self-governing communities. They seek, on a quite different basis from traditional socialism, to supersede capitalist economies and large-scale representative democratic states.[2] But unlike fascists and Stalinists they advocate non-violent means, and seek to prevail by persuasion. The new democratic left, by contrast, is realist; they accept that mass electorates, multi-party competition, a limited number of hierarchically controlled parties, and a territorial state with a monopoly of the means of violence will continue to exist. The aim is to democratize within these parameters. How is this to be done? Two main answers suggest themselves: a 'new republican' tendency based on the idea of 'citizenship', advocating the strengthening of active participation in common, core political institutions and extending the social and political rights of citizens; a tendency more strongly anti-statist, and advocating the crucial role of citizens' initiatives in 'civil society' and relying upon an active organized civil society to act as a check upon and a substitute for the state.[3] These two currents are poles of the same discourse, with crossovers and cross-fertilizations between them. The 'new republican' pole tends to be strong in Britain and the USA; it seeks greater citizen participation and involvement as a means of revitalizing established democratic polities suffering from disillusionment and under-participation by citizens. The 'civil society' pole tends to draw upon the experience of Eastern Europe, where the opposition is compelled to organize outside and against a one-party state. It also draws on the experiences of the 'new social movements' in the West: the ecological, feminist, gay rights, anti-racist, etc., campaigns, which also have either chosen or have been forced to ignore or play down electoral politics in the pursuit of their specific aims.

The difficulty is that to the extent the new democratic left accept the existing representative democratic institutions they must also adapt to their consequences. This they have, in the main, failed to do. Modern representative democracy has predominantly functioned as a means of legitimating governmental power, rather than of making government effectively accountable and open to public influence. It is difficult to see how this could be otherwise outside of situations of extreme crisis where the vote enables the people to veto an unacceptable regime or an authoritarian party seeking power. The problem is that while mass democracy gives the electorate a real power to choose some of the major ruling personnel, it also routinizes and minimizes political participation. The 'new republican' argument for an enhanced role for the citizen and greater participation in common, core political institutions tries to address the failings of modern mass democracy and yet sets its face against them. Limited participation is an institutional feature of mass democracy and not merely a failing due to specific circumstances. Mass electorates and mass parties mean a low level of active participation by the citizens. At best such a democracy permits the masses a vote in periodic and relatively infrequent elections. Active and continuous participation in politics is the choice of the small minority who join political parties and other campaigning organizations.

A mass electorate can only participate infrequently – the cost of frequent campaigning to get in the vote makes regular and routine reference to the people's choice impossible. A mass electorate can only cope with relatively simple choices and so electoral competition tends to reduce itself to a small number of major parties. Representative democratic politics means infrequent and restricted choices for a mass electorate. That is inevitable, even if the vast mass of individual citizens identify with the political process, vote when required and acquire a modest knowledge of politics. When indifference or alienation lead citizens to neglect even the limited duties of mass democratic politics then elections become an even more formal legitimation of those who attain office. In the USA even in the presidential elections only a bare majority of the electorate bothers to vote.

The scope for enhancing the roles of citizens and increasing their level of participation is small. Democratization must rely on something other than higher levels of mass participation. Representative democracy will not work if more than a bare minimum is expected of the demos. In any reasonably stable and moderately prosperous society most people will happily accept their limited participation in and limited knowledge of politics and get on with their own business.

If the participation of citizens in modern mass democracies is limited then, on the contrary, the role of the major political parties is excessive. The major parties are the victors in a process of political competition, having eliminated minor parties and cranks as serious contenders for office. Mass democracy may be a minimal form of political participation for the individual, but it gives the major parties the capacity to monopolize the mainstream political agenda. Hence any political 'alternative' that does not compete for the vote as the parties do and yet seeks to change the political agenda is in danger of political exclusion. It *is* possible to change the agenda, as the green movement has shown, but only to the extent that the major parties adopt and dilute the issues. The major parties survive and, even if they do not prosper, they occupy political space. Thus the PCI in Italy or the Labour Party in Britain may remain out of office for years on end and yet monopolize the space of the possible on the oppositional left of politics. Major left parties shun truly radical reforms in either political or social institutions. On the assumptions that electorates fear radical change and that they fear rear radical *political* change the most, the major opposition mass party of the left will tend to shun genuine radicalism in the hope of office. The dominant opposition mass party limits the scope of effective advocacy of strategies to implement political reform. The new democratic left thus either find themselves shunned by the major left parties or converted into a rhetorical gloss on profoundly conservative reform strategies. Nowhere in the programmes of reform of the new democratic left are the means to displace the mass parties and their stranglehold on mainstream politics canvassed. To do so would be a frontal attack on representative democracy, it would put the new democrats back with the fascists and communists. Yet not to do so largely condemns the advocacy of 'citizenship' and 'republican' activist participation to mere rhetoric. It assures the continuance of left discourse, comforting to intellectuals, perhaps, but not an effective left politics of democratic reform.

Perhaps the emphasis on 'civil society' provides the answer? If limited mass participation in elections and the monopolizing role of the major parties cannot be changed, then perhaps they can be overcome? Political movements for which elections are at best secondary, that operate outside and often against the state, are not constrained by the structural defects of mass electoral democracy. But can they counter those defects and effectively provide a supplement to the limits of the mass democratic political process? One should be careful not to over-generalize the experience of Eastern Europe here, for in the East the state both lacks legitimacy with the broad mass of the people and refuses to concede full representative government. Whilst that continues to be true, then opposition based on 'civil society' can work. Once full representative democracy is conceded and the state is not chronically lacking in legitimacy such strategies of opposition within 'civil society' can have at best local and single-issue effect. In Western representative democracies the state is neither weak nor lacking in the means to legitimate its policies.

State power has grown steadily throughout this century in Western democracies. The state delivers a vast range of vitally necessary goods and services, which the citizens cannot do without. As a public service state it has the capacity to marginalize the 'new social movements' because it reaches deep into civil society. Movements in civil society cannot supplant or occupy the place of the state, precisely because in developed democratic societies civil society is neither homogeneous nor closed against the state. Britain, for example, is not remotely like Poland. Its civil society is diverse, characterized by many competing and contrary interests, and of these interests the 'new social movements' form no more than a minority. Active contest of and attempts to supplant the state by, say, gay activists or black activists in some specific policy sphere or locality are doomed to failure. On the contrary, such movements invariably struggle to influence the major parties and central or local state policy. By reaching into civil society with its 'social' policies, by being open to a degree of influence by those who accept its role, the democratic state can easily prevent a coherent extra-parliamentary opposition. The elements of polyarchy and pluralism in Western democracies work to confine such anti-parliamentarist and anti-statist opposition strategies. Ultimately, activists are bought off by seeking decisions, special programmes, laws or funding from the state.

These arguments may seem pessimistic and to undercut what appears to many on the left as the best hope for political influence through the advocacy of democratic reform. They are not meant to diminish the need for the advocacy of democratization, merely to show the problems with some of the ways the new democratic left have taken it up. Western representative democracies are a curious mixture of success and failure. They succeed on the level of legitimization of governmental authority, but at the price of a low level of citizen participation and a low level of effective accountability of government decision-making. They succeed in part because they demand little of the ordinary elector – minimal effort and minimal knowledge – whilst placing in the hands of the electorate a very real and valuable power of veto. Western democratic institutions cannot be supplanted or challenged head on. The experience of this century leads democratic electorates to fear any party or group advocating some other system than multi-party mass democracy. Representative democracy can only be supplemented, not supplanted. It can only be supplemented in a way that the major parties can accept and that the electorate endorses. That limits radical institutional changes. Representative democracies are conservative; they are generally based on societies where the majority of the people are 'haves', in however small a way. That is why democratic reform is such a difficult cause for the left, despite many assumptions to the contrary.

If one accepts the institutions of representative democracy, how does one seek to counter their failings by new strategies of democratization, and yet deal with the consequences of minimum citizen participation and the dominance of the major electoral parties? The essays in this book are my successive stabs at an answer. This answer has three major themes.

The first theme is the argument that it is possible to use the economic problems of advanced Western countries to enhance democratic influence. If neither centrally planned socialism nor free-market capitalism offer viable strategies for governing the economy, then the alternative can only be economic management through the coordination of the major social interests and through the orchestration of consent through interest group bargaining. That implies the corporatist representation of the major organized interests. The claim made here is that the corporate representation of organized interests can *enhance* democracy, in the sense of increasing public influence over government, and does not undermine it as many critics of corporatism suppose. Corporatism is a threat to democracy only if one supposes there is a single legitimate form of popular representation, elections in territorial constituencies, and that the 'sovereign' state gives expression to the people's will through its legislative and administrative acts. This is to endorse the very features of modern democratic states that are most in need of challenge and the sources of the major failings of representative government.

The second theme is the argument that the concentration of power in centralized 'sovereign' states grossly inflates the problems of democratic accountability, by concentrating information and administrative power, and by increasing the complexity and scale of the means necessary to have influence on decision-making. Corporatism can help to decentralize the state by increasing the role of coordination, bargaining and influence, by mixing the state with civil society, and by building public–private networks of influence and policy-making at central, regional and local levels. Purely political reform is unlikely to be accepted and implemented by the major political parties. The more radical parties may accept political change if it is tied to new strategies for governance of the economy. Economic problems, if they are pressing enough, will lead to institutional innovation. But informal or quasi-formal corporatist arrangements, whilst they are the most immediate practical supplement to representative democracy and a major channel of public influence, cannot entirely counter the problems posed by centralized 'sovereign' state power. Such power, and the parties who govern by means of it, tend to convert formal representative democracy into a means of legitimation. The state and party governments are the main beneficiaries of mass electoral democracy, and they can always use the claim of a democratic 'mandate' to act against or contrary to the informal channels of public influence and quasi-formal corporate bargaining. This is what the Conservative Government has done in Britain since 1979.

Formal constitutional guarantees and the entrenchment in law of civil and political rights are at best a palliative to concentrated 'sovereign' authority. Representative democracy, when combined with hierarchically controlled political parties and concentrated and omnicompetent government in a centralized state, can serve as a means to negate the wider processes of pluralism and public influence and to legitimate the claim to a monopoly of political power. Representative democracy can serve to undercut the wider pluralism of political influence which is the social base of a genuine democracy, in the sense of power constrained by public accountability and public influence. The long-term solution to this problem can only consist in 'pluralizing' the state, that is, making the institutions of the state mirror what Harold Laski called the 'federative' nature of modern society.[4] A 'pluralist' state in the sense used by the English political pluralists, G. D. H. Cole, J. N. Figgis and H. J. Laski, is one in which distinct functionally and territorially specific domains of authority enjoy the autonomy necessary to perform their tasks.[5] It rejects the claim that a single 'sovereign' legislature should possess a plenitude of power, that is, the means to control and define all lesser bodies in society, and the power to undertake and supervise every social task. The 'pluralizing' of the state both reduces the scope of central state power, giving functional, regional and local authorities greater autonomy, and reduces the issues at stake in representative national elections by restricting the role of central government. The most sophisticated forms of pluralism do not aim to abolish representative democracy and replace it by a new single system of functional democracy. Rather they aim to multiply representative bodies and to complement them by forms of functional representation of organized social interests. Pluralism, therefore, gives more room for organized means of influence, representing specific categories of citizens, and it increases the scope for interaction between public bodies and civil society. Pluralism offers a way for the state and civil society to interpenetrate, whilst restricting the scope of state power and its capacity to dominate civil society. Pluralism in this sense creates the space for an active civil society of associations freely formed of citizens and allows those self-governing associations to undertake a greater part of the tasks of social life.

Pluralism in the English sense has traditionally been an anti-collectivist and statist doctrine, but it has always been strongly opposed to the anti-political ideas of communalist direct democracy, to syndicalism, and to Marxist ideas of working-class popular democracy. It denied that society could have a single interest, a single 'general will', or that political power could be concentrated in the hands of one social group or social function. It strongly opposed ideas of Soviet-style 'democracy' or of a state based on the 'workers' power' of factory councils. It argued both for the pluralism of interests and the dispersal of political power. It saw, however, that a pluralist political system needed a public power able to ensure public peace and the rule of law. The public power should be regulatory in function and should regulate but not usurp the power of functional, regional and local authorities.

The third theme concerns the future of socialism as a political theory. The argument advanced here is that socialism can be linked to democratization as a long-term goal, on the one hand, and to new forms of governance of the economy in the shorter term, on the other. Socialism, in this argument, needs to shed the collectivism and statism of central planning and bureaucratically administered welfare. These institutions are only one aspect of the socialist tradition, and they involve a social project at variance with the more libertarian forms of socialism. The claim made here is that 'pluralization' of the state is compatible with the project of associational socialism, with devolving the tasks of social organization and economic activity to self-governing voluntary associations of citizens. Political pluralism creates the space for a civil society of self-governing associations; whereas centralized 'sovereign' state power tends ever more rigidly to restrict that space and to favour hierarchically governed and exclusively owned business corporations closer in nature to its own form of top-down and concentrated authority. Such a socialism, it is argued, is one of the projects possible in a pluralist society with a dispersed and federative form of political power, but that project has to be voluntary and to win support by its own peaceful efforts. A pluralist state and society must include room for projects other than those of socialism, but also the space and scope for socialist institution-building. Socialism must be built in civil society, by voluntary and autonomous efforts. It must return to the associationalist tradition and create its own institutions, in the way that the cooperative movements, the friendly societies and the Arts and Crafts colonies attempted to do. Seeking to monopolize centralized state power, seeking to make socialism a compulsory social project, has been the ruin of socialism.

A fully pluralist state and a society open to associationalist projects must be a long-term objective of democratic socialism. In the shorter term, however, the need to create a collaborative form of governance of the economy provides the basis for both weakening centralized state power and lessening the dominance of the major parties. Only in this way can we hope to move from a representative democracy whose role is increasingly plebiscitarian and legitimatory of established governmental power. The experience of governing the economy by bargaining and the consent of organized interests in the more progressive European states and regions shows the possibility of enhancing pluralism. It shows the possibility of governing the economy, the central task of modern politics, without a high degree of coercion. It shows, through social pacts and organized corporate bargaining, the possibility of achieving a more equitable balance between the state and civil society. This link between long-term aims and shorter-term necessities is developed more fully below in chapter 6.

This argument is undoubtedly controversial and it depends crucially on the willingness of major parties to enter into social pacts to ensure the governance of the economy.[6] The possibility of such pacts is raised and canvassed most fully in chapter 2. The point that needs to be emphasized here is that this argument involves pulling together a number of distinct and often opposed forms of political theory. The answer offered to the problems of representative democracy and the possibility of radical democratization involves being willing to use and to work across a number of distinct traditions in political theory.

Firstly, it involves the utilization and defence of a political theory very unpopular and unfashionable with both the New Right and the new democratic left, corporatism. I argue that corporatism can be both an effective means of relatively non-coercive governance of the economy through bargaining between industry, labour and the state at national, regional and local levels, and a form of representation of organized social interests that enhances democracy, in the sense of greater public influence.

Secondly, it involves the critical use of another unfashionable political theory, at least as far as the left is concerned, American political pluralism. This argument is developed in chapter 3. The claim made here is that American pluralism, specifically in R. A. Dahl's version, allows us to critically understand both the strengths and weaknesses of representative democracy as a form of political competition and in-fluence on governmental decision-making. It is a valuable tool for the critical analysis of Western democratic politics that the left has unwisely spent its time struggling to refute. Properly exploited, it explains why most modern Western democratic countries fail to match up to the standards of measure of an adequately functioning polyarchy.

Thirdly, English political pluralism, a neglected and half-forgotten body of political theory, provides both an invaluable critique of the 'sovereign' state and a way of posing the limitations of the modern forms of left thinking about democratization. This theory is most fully expounded in chapter 4 and chapter 5. The pluralist jurisprudence of Léon Duguit and its relationship to the neo-corporatist political thinking of Émile Durkheim are developed in the latter part of chapter 7.

Fourthly, I have used what may appear to be a wholly alien and opposed form of political and legal theory, that of Carl Schmitt. Schmitt was unquestionably a theorist of the right, a sworn enemy both of English political pluralism and of liberal conceptions of parliamentary democracy. Schmitt may be of the right, his unpopularity and virtual disappearance from political argument in the West stem from his cynical conversion to Nazism, but he has hard and valuable lessons to teach the left. Schmitt figures prominently in chapters 4, 7, 8 and 9. I make no apology for this; Schmitt can legitimately be regarded as the Hobbes of the twentieth century and his ideas are inescapable as surely as his personal politics were repellent. Schmitt shows more clearly than any Marxist what is at stake in state power, how difficult it is to bend the world of politics toward a more consensual and democratic society. He also shows vividly the dangers of political pluralism. Any democratic and pluralist thinking that does not simultaneously seek to learn from him and to find answers to him is mere sloganizing.

I have been compelled by asking these questions to bring these diverse bodies of political thinking together. This combination of theories and thinkers can only be held in tension, brought together because each poses a hard question or offers an answer to one aspect of the problems that we face in developing a democratic theory adjusted to the institutional complexities of institutions and the demands of contemporary politics. Consistency is not to be given preference to explanatory power, nor is it the inevitable concomitant of the latter. Eclecticism is not a virtue, but the creative use of disparate ideas is sometimes a necessity. It would be bogus, moreover, to seek to blend these divergent thinkers and theories into a 'synthesis'. Syncretism is possible only at the level of rhetoric, a conceptual gloss which evades the very real contests and contradictions in these ideas.

One other aspect of the forms of theorizing brought together here needs mention, that is, that I have drawn extensively not only on political but on legal theory. A legal order and the rule of law is a necessary part of any democratic society, and any political theory seeking democratization must show how its proposed institutions are compatible with a sustainable legal order. As in the case of political theory, I have drawn on diverse strands of jurisprudential thinking – these are summarized in chapter 4. In particular legal positivism and its critique by pluralist jurisprudence and by other theories, like Franz Neumann's, are held in tension. Legal positivism remains important precisely because it states the legal claims of the 'sovereign' state, that is, to an unlimited formal law-making power. Laws are what the competent state agencies choose to enact by the appropriate procedures, and the state's unlimited law-making power, even though it remains a claim rather than an attainable fact, is, at least potentially, subversive of the rule of law and the legal order. Lawfulness becomes a merely formal attribute, that laws have been properly enacted. Hence the necessity both to bring other, substantive, standards to judge laws and to deny to the legislature omnicompetence and a plenitude of power. The very accuracy of legal positivism in giving expression to the claims of the modern state helps to highlight the critical role of legal pluralism.

Three issues remain where more discussion is needed than is found in the essays collected here; these are corporatism, the conditions of cohesion in a pluralist society and the place of the state in the international system of states.

CORPORATISM

I have argued below for the importance of corporatist arrangements both for national economic management and for enhancing democratic influence. However, I have made no attempt to utilize corporatism as a means of critique of and an alternative to representative democracy. Corporatism cannot be generalized into a political system without offering a system of representation and accountability as flawed as that of territorial constituencies which directly elect members of the legislature and appoint the heads of government. There is no point in conducting a corporatist critique of representative democracy at the abstract theoretical level, as if corporatism were a better system of representation. Corporatism is a valuable supplement to representative democracy, and it tends to be so because it is expedient for economic management. Corporatism is endorsed here on pragmatic grounds, rather than as a theoretical critique of representative democracy.

The standard corporatist or functional-democratic argument against representative democracy stresses the flaws in such a scheme of representation, that is, that it is actually impossible to represent the wills of the people and that elected assemblies act in the people's name but substitute the wills of the representatives for those of the represented. Functional democracy, by contrast, it is claimed suffers from no such defect since it involves the direct representation of organized interests, where the coincidence between the representative and the active and organized membership of the interest group is very close. A classic expression of this argument is G. D. H. Cole's *The Social Theory*. In fact the critique of 'representation' proves one thing, that there is no 'true' form of representation of the interests of the represented. All schemes of representation involve some element of substitution, and all such schemes have distinct political effects. Representation, whether by function or territorial constituency, is not best analysed by asking how well it 'represents' some set of wills, persons or interests conceived as pre-given to the process of representation. Such questions are ultimately insoluble.

Corporatism cannot thus be defended because its institutional arrangements exemplify 'functional democracy' which is inherently superior to representative democracy. This failure is clear in theory, no less than the advocacy of the replacement of representative by functional democracy would be a non-starter in political practice. Few voters would be impressed to be told that the task of representing their specific functional interests had been given over exclusively to the TUC or the CBI. People would be terrified of losing the vote, quite rightly so. Equally, however, corporatism cannot be attacked by abstract arguments about representation for the very same reason. The claims repeatedly made in the UK that corporatist arrangements 'undermine the sovereignty of Parliament' and that Parliament is truly representative of the people are self-interested. They are typically claims by certain leading parliamentary politicians, whether of the left, like Tony Benn, or of the right, like Lord Hailsham. They are also question begging: is 'sovereignty' desirable, how can parliament be said to 'represent' the people when a majority government can be elected on 42 per cent of the votes cast? Let us leave self-serving politicians aside, and consider the anti-corporatist arguments of a serious and disinterested left political theorist, Noberto Bobbio. In *The Future of Democracy* he argues that functional and corporatist modes of representation are inferior to the territorial for the major processes of national and political representation. He accepts them, however, for the more limited representation within the sphere to which the interests in question are relevant. Thus doctors should be represented in a self-administering hospital, students in a school, but neither doctors nor students have a special claim to be represented as such in a national assembly. There are many pragmatic reasons to oppose an exclusively functional system of representation, but the argument here is against *any* element of explicit functional representation at national level in principle.

Functional representation, despite Bobbio, does have certain merits. Firstly, it brings into the political class persons who are not purely professional politicians. Professional politicians in a representative democracy are highly limited specialists who live off politics and whose primary skill consists in competing for elector's votes. An element of corporate and functional representation would break the domination of national politics by the elected career politician and the permanent official. Such an explicit scheme of representation would also bring into the open the informal corporatism that already exists in the lobbying of elected representatives and officials by organized interests. It would perhaps also give greater legitimacy and influence to those interests whose social importance is not measured by the length of their purse. Bobbio's caution about corporate representation is understandable given his experience of the bogus system of corporate representation in Mussolini's regime and the accompanying denial of any element of free elections for territorial constituencies. But corporatist and territorial representation can be combined in one set of political institutions, a territorial lower chamber being combined with a corporatist senate, for example.

There are problems with creating formally corporatist institutions, however. There is a great danger in corporatist and functional-democratic thinking that it tends to regard certain social interests and certain social groups as being fixed. The functional 'interests' to be represented are taken as givens, with the assumption that the basic order of society is unchanging. By contrast territorial representation is both formal and very flexible: territorial constituencies can be multiplied and expanded, those classes of persons eligible to vote can be changed. Representative democracy can adapt to massive economic and social change, to an unstable and shifting division of labour. Certain corporatist theories cannot build in such flexibility – for example, Hegel's or to a lesser degree Durkheim's. Durkheim, in *Professional Ethics and Civic Morals*, conceives the corporatist intermediaries necessary to the close interaction of state and society as self-governing professional associations. Yet these patterns of representation cannot be fixed, but are at the mercy of a changing occupational structure. Hegel considers the corporations in *The Philosophy of Right* as representing the major orders of a relatively fixed society. Corporate representation under modern conditions cannot be thought of as if the interests to be represented were those of a fixed society of estates. Modern societies are fluid and changing, and functional and corporatist representation, if it is to be effective, cannot be set in too formal or rigid a mould. The open competition of plural groups for influence, with groups and interests rising and falling, is crucial for democracy. Too rigid and formal a corporatism could prevent this.

Formal corporatism raises problems if the aim is to reflect all major organized interests in society in a single assembly. What interests are to count and why? How can we be sure that certain interests are not merely obsolete shells? By the same token the very informal processes of interest group lobbying and bargaining, particularly if the groups are exclusive and pursue only their own particular interests, can therefore undermine democracy. If too formal a corporatism raises problems, too informal a process of interest group representation opens the door to extreme inequality of influence and unfairness of outcomes.

Functional democracy and corporate bargaining look a whole lot more difficult to institutionalize and less unambiguously beneficial than their more naive advocates believe. However, precisely because corporatism is capable of great diversity in both institutional mechanisms and social functions, these defects can be avoided. In particular corporatism does not imply a set scheme of representation, but permits a complex system of consultation and bargaining differentiated by level and issue. Whilst occupational structures do change, the major interests are sufficiently generalized not to be directly threatened by this. Thus the major 'peak' organizations representing management and labour (with perhaps other groups representing small business, farmers and consumer cooperatives – depending on the type of society) are unlikely to be displaced. Moreover, if interest groups are inclusive and bargain to achieve certain agreements over national economic goals then the worst defects of the domination of interest group politics by self-interested exclusive organizations can be avoided.

Interest group representation at 'peak' level and bargaining between industry, labour and the state in national forums are most appropriate for overall national economic coordination, setting macro-economic targets by bargaining and agreement. Such corporatist arrangements are best regarded as quasi-formal. They require institutionalized mechanisms, but not a formal, constitutionally specified corporatist assembly. The purpose of such corporatist forums is not legislation or the direct supervision of government; they are not a parallel national assembly; rather their purpose is consultation, the coordination of economic action, and the bargaining of gains and sacrifices.

Such highly generalized forums representing 'peak' interests are threatened with isolation from and, therefore, little influence over more specific interest groups unless such 'peak' organizations are informed by and can feed into lower-level processes of corporatist consultation and bargaining. It is increasingly clear that regional and local economic regulation is as necessary as that of national macro-economic management, and that the cooperation of public bodies, business and labour is a crucial part of it.[7] 'Peak'-level bargaining will, therefore, be paralleled and informed by equivalent processes at regional and municipal levels, and by the corporate consultation of more specific interests in particular sectors. Such regional, local and sectoral processes are where corporate representation and bargaining can accommodate changing occupational and social interests.

Thus we do not need to have fixed social orders in order to have effective corporatist representation. That would only be true if we see corporatism as performing the same tasks as representative democracy and, therefore, look to create a formal and truly socially 'representative' corporate chamber or assembly. Corporatism should supplement but not supplant representative democracy. It has quite different functions: corporatist forums serve to facilitate consultation (and therefore communication) and coordination (and therefore bargaining) between social interests and public bodies. They serve as channels for the reciprocal influence of governing bodies and those governed. That permits the governed influence and the governors the means of effectively orchestrating policy whilst minimizing coercion. Corporatism, when it works, has many pragmatic advantages; these are adequately expressed in no developed political theory, and, on the contrary, these advantages are masked by some of the theoretical foundations of functional democracy.

The advocacy of a pluralist state which would oversee a pluralist society in which the diverse projects of self-governing associations can be pursued is aimed at those whose libertarian instincts rise against statism and bureaucratic collectivism. Yet it is only credible on certain very special social and political conditions, conditions which have been conspicuously lacking in the over three centuries in which modern state power was built up and consolidated. 'Sovereignty' existed precisely because state agencies needed to be able to make claims on the lives and property of citizens to ensure public peace at home and to protect against rivals abroad. The modern state is the dual product of overcoming the religious civil wars and of pursuing the external wars of national or dynastic interest. Pluralism only makes sense if external threats are removed and if self-governing associations are sufficiently minded to live in peace one with another while in pursuit of their own projects.

A pluralized state and a pluralistic society require a minimum of social consensus and widespread support for certain basic values such as tolerance and respect for the rights of others. Pluralism cannot be sustained without a normative order, and without acceptance of the state's role as regulator of the associations' conduct. Pluralism does not imply that each association or interest may pursue its own course without regard to others. Associations must be aware of their membership of a wider society and the constraints that membership imposes. Pluralism is not a relativistic utopia, in which 'anything goes'. On the contrary the pluralist state would protect the rights of associations and individuals. But the state is no substitute for a political culture in which the majority of political actors subscribe to certain basic and common *mores*; only then can coercion and regulation be minimized to the level compatible with the lesser claims to power of a pluralized state.

Have we any right to expect that actors will or can subscribe to and abide by such *mores*? Certainly, the Rushdie affair should give any intelligent pluralist advocate pause for thought. There are in every modern western country social forces and associations that would ruthlessly exploit the freedoms given them within a pluralist state and yet refuse to accept the rights or legitimacy of others. The more fanatical in the Muslim community offer only a conspicuous example, for there are other more established groups and associations equally likely to abuse such freedom. What forms would such abuse take? Firstly, the attempt to expand at the expense of other groups, and, secondly, the attempt to dragoon and subjugate the individuals who form their members. Totalitarianism is as real a threat when it is the project of an association as when it is the project of a state. The fanatical pursuit of organizational purposes can threaten the social order. Competing groups with different values, for example, Christian religious fundamentalist fanatics who believe gays to be evil and organized gay activities to be struggled against and suppressed, can pose problems for public order as acute as those of the competing confessional groups in the religious civil wars of early modern Europe or the conflict of fascists and communists between the two World Wars. A pluralist society needs a public power capable of ensuring order when adherence to values proves insufficient. It would regulate and limit the forms of competition between groups and associations, and the extent to which groups or associations could exercise control over their members. To do this it would need the power to make law and enforce the rule of law. A pluralist state would not claim the same plenitude of power and legislative omnicompetence as the 'sovereign' state has done, but it would remain a public power and it would ensure a legal order regulating the interaction of groups. A pluralist society would thus inherit both the values of liberalism and the liberal protection of the rights of the individual.

Yet it cannot afford to also inherit those illusions about civil society that developed at the same time as modern liberalism. For almost all Enlightenment thinkers 'civil society' was a wholly positive concept; civil society was the source of enterprise and virtue and could do no wrong. The state, by contrast, if it did not represent and enjoy the consent of civil society, tended towards authoritarianism and corruption. We know, on the contrary, that civil society is not a guarantee of harmony and concord, and that there are many sources of division and antagonism, of which social classes and inequalities of wealth are but one. A pluralist society implies a plurality of social projects, the existence of different values and standards of measure. These can all too easily serve as sources of social antagonism. It is worth remembering, therefore, that there can be worse things than centralized 'sovereign' states. Antagonistic pluralism, where state and society are riven by competing groups, each of which denies co-existence and legitimacy to the other, is worse than a modest measure of authoritarianism on the part of the state. Indeed, as Reinhard Kosselleck argues in *Critique and Crisis*, seventeenth-century thinkers like Bodin and Hobbes envisioned an absolutist state removed from civil society and able to impose its will upon it as a condition of public peace. Civil society was perceived as guilty and a source of corruption of the body politic. The confessional civil wars threatened not just public peace but civilization itself. Only with the social pacification and depoliticization effected both by state policies of religious conformity and religious toleration could civil society come to appear positive and the modern concept of it emerge. When that happened, the absolutist state, separated from and unaccountable to civil society, came to be seen as a source of evil. The Enlightenment critique of absolutism and the modern oppositional critique in Eastern Europe follow a similar logic. This logic is possible only when the critic perceives there to be no pressing enemies without and no danger of civil strife within; the *state* is the main enemy and the main source of civil strife.

We have only to look at Belfast and Beirut to see that this is not an inescapable logic. In both cities most ordinary people dream of a central public power that could ensure civil peace. The point being made here is not that absolutism is either valuable or necessary, but that there are perils in seeking to build a pluralist state and an associationalist society. Associationalism involves the danger of 'communalism', that different social projects will become self-enclosed and self-valuing, encompassing the whole of the life of their members. That is the first step toward antagonistic pluralism. An associationalist society, if it is to survive, requires a widespread commitment by organized social bodies to a common public culture and their active and willing participation in a common public sphere. Tolerance is the first condition for the survival of such a society, that associations recognize and seek not to harm other social groups and social projects. That involves the limitation of the aims of the group which practises tolerance; purging the world of the impure, imposing one's own values as the sole common standards, become impossible aims. Tolerance involves more than the passive acceptance of others, it involves commitments to uphold the public realm and its guarantee that various associational projects will be possible within it. Tolerance is not the indulgence of others, a surrender to their objectives, whatever they may be. It involves a limit and at that limit being prepared to support and aid in the suppression of totalitarian associations and groups in defence of the public realm and the principle of pluralism. I emphasize this apparently illiberal point because too much associationalist and pluralist thinking has been utopian and has subscribed to the Enlightenment prejudice in favour of civil society. No sensible person who looks at the growing religious, value and lifestyle pluralism in the modern West can feel entirely sure that the sources of bitter civil strife are not present in modern civil society. One thing is certain, the image of a central 'sovereign' state able to assure public peace is as much an illusion as that of a pure and harmonious civil society. The threat of civil strife is no argument for centralized state power; the state is too often a party to the conflict, and where it faces an opposed and hostile civil society, as in Poland in the early 1980s, all its supposed strength and 'sovereignty' are insufficient to ensure its position; its very separation from civil society becomes a liability.

THE SYSTEM OF STATES

The most powerful argument for centralized 'sovereign' state power is that it has been the most effective instrument for fighting foreign wars. Such a state can draw most fully on the lives and resources of its people. Less centralized states with less concentrated powers of coercion have been swept aside or overwhelmed in the continuous conflicts since the modern states system developed from the sixteenth century onwards. Until recently the majority of citizens of most states have believed at some time or another that they faced real enemies and in some cases that they would be conquered and subjugated by foreigners they hated. Who can doubt the Poles faced such an enemy in 1939, or that most Germans, whatever they felt about Nazism, supported resistance to the Russians to the very last gasp in 1945? Enemy states can be threatening, even if the regime of one's own state is less than satisfactory.

This pressing reality of enemies and the need to mobilize to fight them has now vanished for the advanced states. Western democracy is secure as it has never been before. Even in 1950 many Western democrats believed that they had to prepare to resist a coming Soviet onslaught. With the economic and political integration of Western Europe, with detente with the Soviet Union, with Japan's continued abstention from an imperial role in Asia, the advanced industrial countries no longer face pressing major enemies. Lesser states may, but they present no threat except to one another; certainly not to First World hegemony.

Yet the condition of the peace the major advanced states have enjoyed since 1945 offers little hope that centralized state power can rapidly become obsolete. Nuclear deterrence has cemented that peace. It has made the risk of major diplomatic and military adventures that they may lead to war between the Superpowers insupportable. Yet it has also cemented political divisions and military rigidities. The world remains much as the victorious Allies carved it up at Yalta in 1945. Even large-scale arms reductions, even the political liberalization of Eastern Europe, will not abolish the two organized armed camps, although these changes will further reduce the danger of war between them.

The modern states system is changing, but it is not crumbling, nor are the respective hegemonies of the Superpowers seriously threatened.[8] That means we shall continue to live in a world of states, with lessened imperatives of military mobilization and greater room for political experiment, but with a strong military-diplomatic constraint remaining on the scope for decentralizing and pluralizing state power. The problem in particular is that nuclear weapons and nuclear technology strongly reinforce centralization, hierarchy and secrecy: in no state is, or could be, the nuclear security apparatus under democratic control.

Deterrence is an ambiguous benefit, it has contributed to the pacification of the advanced world, but it has done so at the price of remote and
yet incalculable risks should it fail and at the price of the concentration
of unaccountable power touching on the matter of life and death for us
all.[9]

Pluralizing the state might thus appear an impossible objective,
prevented by that very states system that stimulated the concentration
of power. Yet there are some grounds for cautious optimism. The
advocacy of a pluralist system in either of the Superpowers is clearly
impossible. Although the USA is a democracy and a formally federal
state, its military power and foreign policy-making are highly concentrated and exclusively controlled. The European Community, however,
is a quite different case. On the one hand, its economic and political
integration can only proceed if it develops a federative and pluralized
structure of government. This will diminish the role of 'sovereign'
national states whilst promoting the authority of functional authorities
within the Community (based on consultation and bargaining) and
promoting the importance of the regional level of government. The new
'social' Europe and the new regionalism are moves in a pluralist
direction. On the other hand, the European Community will not
become an integrated and centralized superstate. Western Europe can
exploit its new relation of detente with the East, and, if it wishes, it can
rely on the 'umbrella' provided by the US deterrent through the states
of the Community's common commitment to the Atlantic Alliance. To
put it crudely, the Europeans can 'export' some of the consequences of
nuclear power, albeit at the price of accepting American hegemony.

If this scenario is at all plausible, Britain is the one country in Europe
least open to such pluralization. Britain has consistently opposed the
political integration of Europe and the further development of Community institutions, and for the reason that this would diminish the
'sovereignty' of the British state. Britain has tenaciously struggled to
remain a nuclear power, despite its relative poverty in the industrialized
world. The imperatives of nuclear security have reinforced what was an
excessively closed, exclusive and unaccountable system of administration. The British Government is also consistently out of step in Europe,
not only in refusing to countenance the enhanced consultation of
organized interests at Community level, but also in rejecting anything
that smacks of 'corporatism' at home. Yet the unpopularity of Britain's
Conservative Government is growing, and the opposition parties increasingly see Britain's isolation from Europe and the new agenda of
integration of Europe as planks in an opposition offensive against the
Government.

Whilst the leading British opposition party, Labour, has switched its
policies on Europe and has adopted a new pragmatism in matters of

nuclear disarmament, it has set its face against the advocacy of institutional reform and major constitutional changes. Labour has not accepted the proposals for constitutional reform advanced by Charter 88, nor is it willing to fully endorse the ideas of the new democratic left.[10] It is also hostile to corporatist strategies for the governance of the economy. This conservatism reinforces my point about the restrictive role of the major radical parties in existing electoral politics. But, in the long run, Labour cannot hope to address the economic and social problems Britain faces without new strategies for governing the economy in general and new ways of building a solid consensus to make the radical and often hard choices necessary to revitalize British manufacturing in particular. It is in terms of these long-term necessities that we have the best chance for institutional changes that will enhance the accountability and openness of government.

2

Representative democracy and its limits

Democracy is the dominant idiom in political discourse in Britain, as in all other Western countries. Everyone is a democrat irrespective of their other political views and anyone with the slightest concern for political success carefully avoids criticizing democracy for fear of the political wilderness. Representative democracy is such a powerful tool of legitimation of the actions of government that no serious politician, even if they have just lost an election, will question it. Democracy is an unquestionable good and representative democracy is identified with democracy. To challenge the dominant idiom appears to be political suicide, but such a challenge needs to be mounted in the name of democracy. The dominant idiom – representative democracy as democracy – in fact serves to legitimate modern big government and to restrain it hardly at all. Electoral victory serves as a means to stifle other claims to political competition, public pressure and governmental accountability; it permits government to deny challenges to their authority which may in fact be necessary if government is to be made more effective and accountable. The following discussion is not an anti-democratic attack on representative democracy, but rather a criticism of its capacity to do the job it is supposed to do: supervise, restrain and control big government. Part of the argument is that corporatist mechanisms of consultation and bargaining are a vital supplement to representative democracy in the era of big government and organized social interests. Corporatism, it is claimed, would strengthen rather than weaken democracy in the UK and assist in the solution of the problem of Britain's economic decline.

Despite democracy being the dominant political idiom most politicians and ordinary citizens are unclear as to the nature and the purpose of democracy as a political mechanism. The term 'political mechanism' may appear odd, but it enables us to treat political institutions in terms of their functions and outputs.[1] If one asks people – 'what is democracy and what is it for?' – most of them are puzzled. They tend to treat democratic institutions as an unquestioned fact of obvious utility, as an ultimate value or as an end in itself. 'What do you mean, what is it for?' 'Democracy is obviously a good thing, how can you question it, just look at the places that do not have it?' And so on. But all political mechanisms are a means to *do* something, for example, to produce certain sorts of decisions or to mobilize resources for certain objectives. After some more questioning one usually gets an answer like, 'to give expression to the will of the people'.

What can that mean? In a sense the answer has an obvious meaning: democracy is a decision procedure and the people who use this political mechanism to choose those public actions they want done by government. But there are a mass of problems in this obvious meaning. For a start, democracy is presented as a single idiom: one is a democrat, one is in favour of democracy. But once one starts to ask what democracy is for, one uncovers the thorny problem of what democracy is. There is no 'democracy' in the singular, rather there are a variety of doctrines of democracy and a variety of political mechanisms and decision procedures which are claimed to be democratic.

Let us begin in our quest to unravel this idiom presented in the singular with one of the simplest and most obvious definitions, that given by the *Oxford English Dictionary* as 'government by the people'. Democracy is a form of government or rule. In its simplest form it is the direct rule of the people themselves as a body without superior authority set over them. Such a direct democracy necessitates that 'the people' are very few (a few thousands of citizens at most), that the tasks of government are simple and do not require special training or continuous attention, and that the political body in question stands against all the world and recognizes no higher authority. Such a democracy today is inconceivable today. It became obsolete in Europe in the fourth century BC for the simple reason that tiny self-governing statelets could not compete militarily with larger more complexly governed powers. If direct democracy is taken seriously today it can only be in a different sense as a means of management of some relatively simple and stable activity within a larger political whole. It will always be a subordinate form of administration within a bigger system of government which is not itself directly democratic. Direct democracy should not be despised. Where appropriate as a level of administration, it tends to be cheap, efficient and it gives those members interested enough to be active in it great confidence which stems from a good training in basic administrative-political skills. But it can never be a doctrine appropriate to the main forms of modern politics.

The *Oxford English Dictionary* follows its bald initial definition thus: 'That form of government in which the sovereign power resides in the people as a whole and is exercised either directly by them (as in the small republics of antiquity) or by officers elected by them'. The *Oxford English Dictionary* thus treats direct and representative democracy as if they were varieties within a species. But they are different in kind, as Max Weber pointed out when he noted that the former is a type of rule while the latter is actually a form of legitimation of rule.[2] The *Oxford English Dictionary* definition is interesting not because it embodies some special wisdom or authority about political concepts but, on the contrary, because it engages in the slippage absolutely characteristic of modern everyday democratic vocabulary, that is, to identify representative democracy with rule by the people. Lincoln's Gettysburg Address has the formula precisely, representative democracy is 'government of the people, by the people and for the people'. In the nineteenth century, the slippage was comprehensible because autocratic monarchy and oligarchic rule based on wealth and privilege were still the predominant forms of Western politics – democracy in this context could mean rulers chosen from among formally equal citizens by some mechanism in which all these citizens could equally participate. But even so, by any stretch of the imagination, it could not mean rule *by* the people.

Let us consider the doctrines of popular sovereignty and representative government, not as espoused by any particular political theorist but at the *OED* level of public political discourse. Political authority is presented as a delegated power brought into existence by the expressed will of the people. I do not mean here some explicit doctrine of a social contract, but the implication of the claim that the sovereign power ultimately resides in the people and that the form of government gives expression to the will of the people. The ultimate sovereign power must be given expression in some representative body to which that power is delegated. The national assembly or parliament is 'sovereign' because it expresses the delegated power of the people and it is legitimately so because it is 'representative' of the people's will.

The assembly or parliament is a sovereign legislature that makes laws that take the form of universally applicable general rules, which single out or disadvantage no individual citizen or group of citizens. The assembly then delegates a portion of its own power to an administrative apparatus in order to give execution to and to enforce these laws. The executive portion of the democratic government is answerable to the legislative assembly or to the judiciary as interpreters and guardians of the law. The sovereign will of the people expressed through the assembly and its laws will infringe the basic liberties of none of the citizens because these laws are universally applicable to all, and the people as a whole will not consent to infringe those inalienable rights which they each possess as individuals. The delegated power of execution and enforcement must put that legislation into effect *sine ira et studio*, therefore, it cannot damage the liberties of the law-abiding. If the executive does act in an arbitrary or partial way then it will be called to account by the assembly. Representation guarantees that the legislature expresses the will of the people, who cannot wish to harm themselves, and the doctrine of the answerability of the executive to the legislature ensures that the delegated power of government is not abused. Democracy and the rule of law are thus fully compatible.

Doubtless, when put in this form, most people recognize such ideas as the bland evasions of elementary civics courses. The commonplaces of democratic political legitimation are the main themes of not-yet-defunct classical political theory. In fact they are still the substance of the popular doctrine of democracy prevailing in the West. Only by means of such classic archaisms can representative government appear today as democratic rule, as giving genuine effect to the will of the people. Stated thus baldly the doctrine must appear incredible as a description of our political system to any person even casually acquainted with the workings of that system. But, incredible or not, it remains the dominant idiom of modern politics. Stated in the form above the doctrine of representative democracy involves grave contradictions and grossly implausible assumptions when set beside the actualities of modern politics.

Several basic contradictions are built into the doctrine. They may appear 'obvious' to any even competent political scientist, but 'stating the obvious' has its value. The commonplace level of political discourse, where the legitimation of existing institutions is politically effective, carries on in sublime disregard of academic political science and abstract political theory. The legitimation of existing institutions of representative government as 'democracy' *tout court* is an obstacle to the perception of the need for reforms to make modern government more accountable and, therefore, more effective. The contradictions between representative democratic doctrine and modern governmental practice need to be registered *politically*, for however 'obvious' they may be to the academy, they have not registered with most politicians or voters.

The first of these contradictions is the most important and that is, that it identifies a decision-procedure for selecting political personnel with one for selecting policies or laws. In choosing the one the people choose the other. But it is assemblies or parliaments which make laws and governments that make decisions and not the people. The electors choose some of the personnel involved in making the governmental decisions, but they cannot directly choose the decisions. The electors may reject personnel who submit themselves for re-election as representatives for the choices they *have* made but always relative to some very limited set of alternative personnel and on the basis of no more than suppositions about the choices they in turn *may* make. Politicians can always plead changed circumstances, constraints on decision-making beyond their control or the unanticipated consequences of legislation or action when explaining why they failed to do what they promised or when what they promised turned out badly. A mass of investigations in political science show that voters do not pay much attention to the specific policy 'promises' of parties. Voters pick and identify with parties and party leaders, and they are usually ill informed about the actual policy proposals of the parties. In practice, voters understand the game far better than the prevailing doctrine of representative democracy would lead them to; they pick parties and people and do not attempt to 'pick' policies or decisions. At best the electorate rejects those politicians it deems to have failed but its choice of alternatives is always limited to a very small number of organizations. An election is not a pure expression of the people's will but a choice between a small set of organizations, i.e. political parties.

The second contradiction stems from the idea that laws are general rules and because they are universally applicable they cannot infringe individual rights. The doctrine assumes that what the legislature does is pass general laws and that the executive is no more than an impartial agency of enforcement of those laws. As we have seen, the legitimating use of the notion of the rule of law supposes laws to have received genuine democratic assent, to apply to all citizens as norms for conduct and to be fair. Actually most legislation consists in delegating powers of decision and action to executive agencies, that have the derived power to make such rules as necessary and administer an activity as they see fit within some broad statement of objectives. Laws are less universal norms regulating conduct than legal sanction for specific administrative measures. Likewise, in the doctrine government is supposed to possess a doubly delegated authority, from the people to the legislature and from the legislature to government. In practice, government is a continuing agency divising policies and pursuing objectives, and it is also a party government. Far from being a servitor of the legislature, government is the initiator of legislation: the legal requirements necessary for the policy programmes of civil servants and senior party members are brought to the legislature and carried through it by means of party discipline. The members of a party government must take a great deal of the continuing policy and decision-making initiated within the government's administrative machine as given; it can initiate, alter or superintend only a small fraction of it. Party rule means the governmental direction of the legislature; parties are an instrument of patronage and discipline controlled by the leading party figures in the government. The legislature typically carries through a governmentally sponsored legislative programme extending the specific powers of action of the government and, although shaped by various forces, embodying some of the objectives of the party leaders. The actualities of continuing government and party government thus reverse the positions of legislature and executive. Legally sanctioned governmental rule-making and action is far from being universally applicable; it is often specifically targeted at definite groups to their benefit or detriment.

The third contradiction is that 'representation' is a circular process; there is no way of judging how representative of the people one particular scheme is without comparing it to another. There is no pure form of representation, only definite packages of political mechanisms: voting systems, means of determining constituencies, degrees of suffrage, types of assembly, laws governing parties, etc. These packages have very different political consequences. To challenge one package as 'unrepresentative' is always to measure it, even if implicitly, against some other. Proportional representation is widely claimed to be better than our current first-past-the-post system in the UK, because it enables the number of representatives in Parliament to correspond more closely to the votes cast for the parties. But the scheme proposed some time ago by the Liberals, for example, favours parties which obtain a substantial portion of the votes in a constituency. It means that a party may receive, say, 5 per cent of the vote nationally and receive no seats. Again, why should representation for a national party depend on constituencies which often favour one party by reason of the way the boundaries are drawn and which can vary by as much as 20,000 electors in size? A national party list and the requirement that a party obtain no more votes than the current average number of votes in a constituency in order to obtain one MP would surely be more representative? But would national politics be more representative of the 'people's will' if, as a consequence of such a national-list system with such low qualifying quotas, coalition governments were to be endlessly formed and reformed from the leaders of perhaps a dozen parties and on the basis of bargaining to which the people cannot be privy? I happen to favour the principle of PR but I have no illusion that the various possible schemes will act evenly on electors or parties. Whatever happens, PR or not PR, the electors will never be able to choose decisions or policies, only personnel and parties.

It might be objected that not only are these criticisms obvious, they are also pointless. Does the doctrine really matter if the system works? Who could seriously imagine that it would be possible actually to represent in government decisions the wills of electors, when these are diverse, changing and contradictory? It is difficult to believe that many people can be happy with the fact that the supposed theory of the representative democratic system is so far at variance with its practice.

Once one problematizes the notion of 'representation' then modern democracy ceases to be a form of delegated rule *by* the people and instead becomes a form of rule by professional politicians and government officials *over* the people, in which some of those rulers are periodically changed by the mechanism of election. The standard commonsense response to such criticism is: 'better a system in which personnel are thus subjected to the threat of change and in which the electors have a choice between at least two parties than one in which neither of these things happens'. Yes, indeed, far better. But that is not the point. If we compare a system where there are at least minimal processes of political competition and, therefore, some political choices, with one in which they are absent, the issue is not in doubt. Better a very defective system of representative government than the best autocratic government. This comparison induces complacency, and appears again to make 'democracy' an unqualified political good, an end in itself. But this is wholly by virtue of comparison with a form of rule not subject to political competition, public scrutiny or public influence.

So what is democracy for? It can only be, once we have cleared away the myths of rule by the people, a set of political mechanisms for ensuring the benefits of political competition, public scrutiny and public influence. These benefits are that governmental decisions be responsive to the needs of citizens, efficient because based on adequate information and subject to criticism, and not systematically oppressive of individuals. To talk in this way is to assume a government machinery which would otherwise start to behave very differently if it were not subject to such constraint. It is to recognize the existence of large-scale continuing government and to accept that it is not a mere device for executing the 'will of the people' but stands in authority over the citizens. In this sense 'democracy' becomes a set of political mechanisms, of which representation through elections is one, that exercise constraints on government but is not itself a form of popular government.

To talk in this way is radically to undercut the idea of democracy as government by a sovereign people, whether directly or through representatives. It is to pose modern government as a problem and not as a mere expression of the people's will. An important current of nineteenth-century liberalism did, indeed, perceive government as a problem, the less of it the better and the less it interfered with the rights of the individual the better. Constitutionalist liberalism sought to fetter the actions of government, but it also tended to oppose democracy. Conservative liberals opposed widening the electorate to include all classes of the adult population and also the legalization of such mass agencies of political pressure as the trade unions. They did so because they feared that the 'people' would demand forms of action by the government which would take the administrative machinery of state into areas where it threatened the rights of the individual, in particular the right to private property. Some conservatives feared that mass pressure for reforms would lead to such a growth of the governmental machine that it could no longer be controlled or superintended by a handful of parliamentary notables. On both counts they were right, according to their own values, and yet their opposition was futile. The conservative liberal response was doomed not merely because it set itself against the masses but also against government agencies and official perceptions of the need for the state action to assure the working of a complex industrial society. The calendar could not be kept at 1831 for ever. The liberal anti-governmental protest constantly re-emerges, as in Lord Hailsham's campaign for a Bill of Rights during the previous Labour Government. Mrs Thatcher's administration may use liberal anti-statist and free-market rhetoric, but its objective is to change the direction and the policies of big government, not to abolish it.

Big government is the creature of a large-scale and complex industrial society. In such a society, whether capitalistic or socialistic, the state must provide social and economic regulation and management; it must also directly deliver a host of necessary services. Big government exists and it will not go away. Fashionable Conservative remedies which drastically reduce the scope of state action in order to enhance the public's choice are in no sense an enhancement of democratic control.

There are two main reasons for this:

1 Reducing what is done in the name of the state matters not one whit if the tasks are taken on by large-scale private corporate bureaucracies, organizations which dwarf many nineteenth- and twentieth-century states. In that case we merely substitute even less accountable big private government for big public government.
2 The loss of public provision in health, education and welfare makes a significant proportion of the people less and not more able to influence public affairs. A healthy, well-informed and secure population is more likely to pay attention to the doings of government than an ill-educated one living in fear of the doctor's bill or the sack.

It is now radicals and liberals, not Lord Hailsham, who hanker after a Bill of Rights. They see it as a means of checking governmental power. Proposing formally to endow citizens with 'rights' by law, to prevent the infringement of the 'private' sphere by the state, is to try to remain in the early nineteenth century. It relies on an external 'check' upon government rather than on the transformation of governmental practices. It is a remedy *after* abuse of power, not a continuing control on the use of power. Moreover, it would be difficult today to claim that there can be any 'inalienable' rights for the individual in the strict sense, since the necessities of economic management, public health, social welfare and social control make the degree of regulation of individuals a matter of policy debate and public convenience.

If the dominant conception of representative democracy as public control remains marooned in the nineteenth century and big government cannot be superintended on 'our' behalf by a handful of ministers and MPs then we need to think again about our doctrine of democracy and the institutional framework of democracy. The constitutionalist liberal may propose obsolete remedies and may wholly misconceive the nature of modern government, but the objective of subjecting government to control and review – even if it is now that of the 'total' rather than the 'nightwatchman' state – is not absurd. One thing is certain, we cannot place an undue reliance on representative democracy in doing so.

Representative democracy has the limited virtue of enabling certain of the leading decision-making and policy-initiating personnel in the state to be changed periodically or be threatened with change. This should not be overestimated as a means of control. Firstly, our present system puts party leaders at the head of an hierarchical administrative machine; whilst limited in their capacities of control and supervision, they have the capacity to intitiate policies over a period of years and push a number of them through. Representative democracy permits party government legitimated by a popular vote, but that vote may 'represent' the choices of a minority of the active electorate. Most party leaders are complicit with big government and do not in practice favour the closer superintendence and control of its actions by 'outside' political forces because this would restrict their own capacity for action. Party leaders are seeking to be the heads of an 'elective despotism' to use Macaulay's phrase. Secondly, parties can use their governmental position to extend and secure their rule: this can take mild forms such as choosing a favourable time for declaring an election or engineering one with, for example, a consumer spending boom, or less mild ones such as blatant gerrymandering, disqualification and harassment of voters, barring opposition parties, etc. Elected governments in multi-party systems may rule for decades at a time, in some cases because they are successful and popular such as the Swedish Social Democrats, but in other cases elections amount to no more than a farce from which the government claims legitimacy as expressing the 'people's will'.

Once we stop contrasting representative democratic political competition with the political processes of a closed bureaucratic autocracy we begin to see that the election of a limited number of personnel to government is like the periodic change in the top management of a large continuing enterprise: policies may change but the basic structure of authority remains. The real issue is to change the regime of business as usual in big government, without imagining we can simply turn it into small government.

But why is there a problem? It is not British government wholly unlike the corrupt, arrogant and authoritarian bureaucracies in some other states? Yes, but surely nobody is going to be satisfied because we do things better than a banana republic. There are some very real problems with our present system of control of government which makes it fall far short of an adequate 'democracy' in the sense of a political system in which the state is sufficiently responsive to public influence and debate about policy measures. There are four main areas of concern.

1   One, as outlined above, is the tendency of representative democracy to turn into the 'elective despotism' of party government; politicians, far from being a primary defence against the governmental machine, exploit its potentialities of centralized and hierarchical administration to the full to drive through a limited number of their own objectives.

2   Big government is, however, so big that a handful of party leaders and ministers cannot directly control or superintend more than a tiny percentage of decisions and so along with the elective despotism of party government goes the largely unaccountable rule of the official.

3   The combination of party government and continuing official administration and policy initiation leads to a double pressure toward secrecy and the control of policy information. The party leaders want an administration which is loyal and responsive only upwards and which reveals only those aspects of policy or the information pertaining to it which suit the government's political purposes. The officials in turn pursue long-term departmental policies and this leads to the rule of the unelected official not only in matters of routine or detail but in major issues that either never come before elected representatives or only before a small number of senior ministers on a 'need-to-know' basis and with very strong pressure to pursue official policy. It is in 'national security' matters of such vital importance as to require widespread debate and which ought to be subject to the widest range of political pressures that this rule of secrecy and officialdom is most evident.

4   Big government is now so big that it is difficult for a ministerial cabinet or governmental party pursuing a programme of policy change to coordinate effectively policy over a number of departments and policy areas. This is partly a function of administrative 'drag' but also of the existence of a number of quite different 'departmental views' some of which will contradict the overall policy, and the upshot is that it is difficult to pursue large-scale programmes of social and political change, certainly within the lifetime of one parliament.

The result is a governmental system that grows by accretion, that is secretive and unresponsive, and difficult to direct toward large-scale objectives in the face of rapidly changing circumstances. Britain's system of government is widely recognised to be bad in these respects compared to many of our European neighbours, but this seldom seems to register with British mainstream politicians as a serious threat to democracy. What makes our situation particularly problematic is that it is less easy simply to pursue 'business as usual' in government because of the extent of our economic decline and the social strains it has brought in train. We do need large-scale social and economic changes to remedy this decline and such changes are very difficult to get out of the present system of dual government by parties and officials. Party government leads to the illusion of decisive action. Between 1963 and 1979 a succession of governments promised to modernize Britain effectively, according to their own perceptions of the causes of its economic decline and prescriptions for a remedy. These successive governments changed the policies for their predecessors in some important matters, but then came to grief at the polls and found their own policies being changed in turn. From 1979 onwards we have had a prolonged period of Conservative government, but only the appearance of consistency in economic policy. Policy has shifted pragmatically with circumstances and with the needs of maintaining office. Mrs Thatcher quietly buried full-blooded monetarism, and discovered 'electoral Keynesianism' in time for 1983 and strongly revived it for 1987. What Conservative rule has not done is to reverse Britain's economic decline. What Mrs Thatcher has done is to reinforce the authoritarian tendencies of British party government. The Conservatives have also gradually made peace with officialdom, having partly re-shaped it in their own image. A successor government of different persuasion will certainly find itself confronted with the 'departmental view'. But if it continues the disastrous tradition of party government it will face more difficulties than the resistance of officials.

Any party seeking social change needs both to make government more accountable to and more responsive to society as a whole. This may seem a paradox, surely social change is best driven through from the top? But successive British governments, even those derided as pursuing 'consensus' by Mrs Thatcher, have only mobilized the support of a fraction of society for a task that needs the support of the vast majority, the reversal of Britain's economic decline.

Making government more continuously accountable to and responsive to public debate and public pressure may actually help to make the process of policy formation and execution more consistent and effective. Parties, because they are periodically subject to electoral contests, tend to 'buy off' selected groups, this is one of the dominant and most successful channels of public influence. But it is a discontinuous one and can have disastrous consequences on policy, as the process of accommodation of electorally influential national and local lobbies in the USA shows. Britain has its own equivalent in the middle-class subsidy state: mortgage interest relief, company cars, occupational pensions, etc. What party would dare to challenge this welfare state for the well-to-do? Such a process of concession and accommodation of influential interest groups is perfectly consistent with a virtual absence of public scrutiny over or influence upon other major policy issues and areas. The sociologist Emile Durkheim defined democracy not in terms of a set of representative institutions but as a condition of effective mutual interaction based on adequate information between the state and civil society.[3] My argument so far has been that in practice representative democracy does not secure this interaction to a sufficiently satisfactory degree and that the doctrine of representative democracy widespread among politicians and the public in Britain enables this failure to continue. The symptoms of failure are recognized but not the cause. Party politicians in particular have too great an interest in the present system to wish either to comprehend it or to change it.

At this point I am obliged to offer some remedies. Let me begin, however, by saying what I do *not* propose. Firstly, it would be foolish to imagine that we can abandon the mechanism of representative democracy or completely abandon the institution of party government. Most people would greatly fear losing the vote; at least it offers some constraint on the actions of government. Political parties are an inevitable consequence of mass electoral democracy; they are vote-getting bureaucracies, and parties also organize political opinion to the point where elections become relatively simple matters of choice between a small number of alternatives. Just as the electorate needs the relatively simple choices offered by party images because it is neither well enough informed about or involved in politics, so we can see why more 'populist' proposals for making government responsive to the people are a non-starter. Referenda, for example, offer the spurious hope of a 'people's choice'. They are ideal tools for government or influential lobbies to acquire legitimacy for a policy or an institution. Most of the populist proposals for the reform of representative democracy are devices for the political mobilization of opinion-fed masses by the elite. Populist politics generally wants to short-cut informed debate and opinion by a simple yes or no vote; Proposition 13 put to the electorate of the State of California is a very good example of the complex consequences of an issue being hidden in a simple and apparently attractive proposal to cut state taxes.

Populism is the enemy of the informed control of big government because it relies on the empty category of the 'people'. Western societies are democratic to the extent that they are, not simply because they have free elections and the choice of more than one political party, but because they permit effective political competition and debate. Not only parties but a plurality of trade unions and other corporate interest organizations, special issue campaigns, etc., compete to influence decisions. Representative democracy can actually be used to legitimate action against this pluralism; increasing the centralization, hierarchy and closedness of state administration the better to give expression to party government. Reducing the capacity of independent action by non-state organizations like trade unions can be justified by the claim that only central government is fully democratic because only it fully expresses the people's will. Exactly the same justification as that used by the Jacobins in the French Revolution is being used by Mrs Thatcher's Government today.

If we want a more democratic society we need more effective and widespread political competition and debate, not an elective despotism claiming authority from a popular vote. How do we obtain this and how do we at the same time obtain greater continuity in policy and coordination between policy areas? There is no contradiction between seeking competition and seeking continuity, if that competition is public, continuous and arrives at a measure of consensus. Democracy's future at the national level rests less on the choices of individual voters than on the effective representation of organizations representing major social interests. Effective influence on government depends on organization. But organized interests can act in different ways and some of the outcomes, whilst exhibiting strong political competition, do not ensure coordination or continuity in policy. Interests can be pursued singly and exclusively, with organizations lobbying for concessions and advantage over others. That this can lead to a virtual Balkanization of national politics and the growth of a political culture obsessed with getting a good deal for one's own interest can be seen in the contemporary USA. An effective progress of democratic competition between organized interests is one in which they bargain corporatively, collectively and cooperatively in association with the state. In Sweden, for example, the leaders of industry, labour and the state have bargained in this way for much of the post-War period and generally with considerable success. There is no reason why such corporate bargaining should be restricted to tripartite determination of wage levels and other components of macro-economic policy, or why much broader social interests should not be included in a more formally corporative political system. For example, it would be possible to replace our present House of Lords with a corporatist second chamber. Such a continuously functioning chamber would permit continuity, consensus and coordination in policy – a programme which could pass such a chamber would have a much higher chance of lasting than any proposal of a party government.

Corporate organizations are, in turn, effective only if they say what their members will in fact be able to do and if the members are disciplined enough to do what their interests organizations say. Accepting a bargaining process and the need for continued compromise, taking an active interest in one's organization and obeying it are the preconditions for corporate democracy. The norms and attitudes underlying such a democracy are less strong in the UK than in some European countries like Sweden or Austria or West Germany. Perhaps if we all stopped imagining that 'our' party government will enable us to turn the corner out of economic decline after the next election we might start to think differently.

Corporatism has received a very bad press in Britain, from both academics and politicians. The reasons have less to do with the intrinsic limitations of corporatism than with the severely limited forms of corporatist bargaining practised in Britain and public attitudes toward them. Corporate bargaining in Britain has been restricted in its agenda, largely to wage freezes, has been confined to a narrow range of 'peak' organizations with poor control over their members, and has been widely perceived by both left and right as an undemocratic makeshift undermining the sovereignty of Parliament, and, therefore, democracy. In other countries the agenda has been wider, the bargaining continuous rather than a matter of emergencies, the organizations represented more inclusive and more disciplined, and public attitudes more positive, accepting policy based upon bargaining and corporatist representation as vital mechanisms of democratic influence.[4]

A system of political competition and bargaining in which corporate organizations play a major part has less need of a highly centralized and hierarchical state than one dependent on party government for its 'democratic' component. Party government wants the state to be responsive to it and therefore subordinate and coordinated in its action. A more pluralistic system of government, where distinct dimensions of authority representing different functions have more political autonomy, could be the outcome of a system in which government programmes enjoy wide consensus. Officials in a less hierarchical and more pluralistic system could be more open and 'political', more accessible to public debate because less concerned to hide things from or to please superior officials or politicians. One way to counter big government is to 'pluralize' it into its component functions. There is less risk of lack of coordination of and continuity in policy if these are then provided by a continuing process of corporate bargaining across a broad range of interests.

The UK is a much more centralized state than most of its European neighbours and it is also a country with the weakest processes of open corporate bargaining. This is not to say our neighbours' political systems are without fault or that they too do not subscribe to the notions of representative democracy I outlined and criticized at the beginning. Few of them, however, expect so much of party government or give that government so much of the work of democracy to do. That British parties have been a major source of the growth of centralized government should come as no surprise, that they should have been considered as its primary means of control ought to shock us. We should also be shocked that we have made so little progress in the political theory of democracy since the eighteenth century. Our democracy has been gravely weakened by this complacent archaism; it may be weakened still further if we do not do something soon and change the mental habits that lead to inaction.

Corporatism is now thoroughly out of favour across a good deal of the British political spectrum. Labour has no love of it and fears even to test the good will of the unions, favouring loose agreements rather than bargaining leading to binding norms. The Conservatives regard corporate bargaining as anathema, part of the wretched era of 'consensus' politics that nearly brought Britain to its knees. Bargaining between organized interests is seen as a weak alternative to vigorously pursued central government policy by both Labour and the Tories. The problem is that bargaining is essential when the government requires widespread cooperation and consent to attain certain objectives. The Conservatives seek to avoid this by a *dirigiste* policy in the public sector, by privatization, and by supporting the authority of private managements to manage. Labour has less of a clear governmental doctrine, but the Labour left has traditionally favoured directive planning for business and autonomy in collective bargaining for the unions. Each party favours great autonomy for its own organizations and strict, legally enforced orders for those on the other side. This places an intolerable burden on democratic legitimation in order to sustain the government making such policies. It relies heavily on the legitimacy of its 'mandate' and thereby weakens representative democracy, by identifying it with policies which significant social interests regard as inescapably partial.

The problem would not be so serious had Britain's economic decline been checked by the longish period of Conservative rule. However much the Government had abused its (minority) democratic mandate, it could claim justification in having delivered the goods. The enthusiasts for the Thatcher experiment boast of Britain's economic strength, yet industrial output is barely higher than in 1979 (and below 1973), the underlying trends in the balance of trade in manufactures are distinctly unfavourable, and levels of investment in manufacturing remain unsatisfactory.[5] The long-term implications of these facts are serious indeed. We are currently suffering balance of payments deficits even at the peak of UK oil production. Unemployment remains unacceptably high and poverty is widespread. To tackle these problems at root requires something different from clever economic policies driven through ruthlessly by a government claiming legitimacy from an electoral victory (on the basis of a minority of the electorate). It does not matter whether that government is Conservative or Labour. There are no specially 'smart' economic policies in our situation, certainly not ones that ignore or railroad major social interests. In fact, the key to broadly based economic recovery and industrial renewal is political change, change that leads to a real and widespread commitment to get things done. To tackle mass unemployment, poverty and industrial decline citizens will have to sacrifice short-term advantages and accept a considerable measure of redistribution of national income from consumption to investment. This is just what the UK political system has failed to orchestrate.[6] A long-term commitment of broad sections of the population through their organizations to substantive economic goals rather than to immediate benefits appears remote and to expect it naive. Which is another way of saying that it has had weakly developed processes of corporate bargaining and has failed to make corporatism a central part of democracy.

3

Retrieving pluralism

The title of this chapter may appear a curious one to any mainstream
political scientist or political theorist. Who could imagine that pluralist
theory had become so neglected or buried in intellectual obscurity that
an effort was needed to recover it? Well, one only has to look at the
radical and Marxist criticism of pluralism to see that an effort of
recovery is needed. A retrieval is necessary to preserve for the left the
valuable tools of analysis and means of social criticism contained in the
work of some of the pluralists. By and large pluralist arguments have
been lost on the left. They see pluralism as at best a grotesque
mis-description of the realities of power in the Western capitalist
system. Others, less charitable, see it as an account so at variance with
the facts that it must be an ideological apologia. The pluralists see power
as relatively widely diffused in Western industrial countries in which
representative democracy exists, and in a few other cases such as India.
But the reality, it is claimed, is domination by a capitalist ruling class or
a military-industrial power elite.

Pluralism is thus treated as a hypothesis about the nature and
distribution of power in advanced capitalist democracies. This hypothesis is found wanting on a number of counts. Firstly, it ignores the
systematic inequality in the distribution of income and wealth characteristic of such societies. At the very least this leads to a discrepancy in the
political resources available to different classes of actors: money, time,
knowledge and organizational skills. As one might expect, political
participation and political influence are very unevenly distributed, with
the poorest largely silent, inactive and therefore unheard. Secondly, it
concentrates on surface features of the political system – actual decision-
making and attempts to influence it by political actors. This takes place
on the basis of the effective, if *de facto*, exclusion of a large part of the
adult citizens and a consensus among those competing to influence

decisions about what are the outer limits of forms of political action, the issues entering into politics and the possible range of outcomes. A society of unequal influence leads to a decisive control by the minority of active and influential citizens over the content of the political agenda – certain issues never appear there and never come to be matters of decision despite their importance and their salience to the interests of large numbers of other citizens. Pluralism has a 'one-dimensional' view of power.[1] Against it radicals like Peter Bachrach and Morton Baratz, in 'Two Faces of Power', *American Political Science Review* (1962), argue the thesis of the 'mobilisation of bias', the ability of powerful actors and associations to control the political agenda. Thirdly, Marxists and other radical critics like Lukes, in *Power*, find even this 'two-dimensional' view of power wanting. The Marxists see the control of the agenda as the result not merely of the actions of particular powerful political agents but of the very capitalist system itself – its political structures and dominant ideology work to exclude certain questions and issues by their very nature. Fourthly, critics like C. Wright Mills, in *The Power Elite* (1956) and Ralph Miliband, in *The State in Capitalist Society* (1969) argue that the state is a continuing stable policy-making agency largely unaffected by electoral contests or political campaigns. The members of the top military, political and business elites share a common view of the world based on a common economic and educational background – for Mills they are the power elite, for Miliband the ruling class. Power is hierarchical, exclusively possessed and exercised in a continuous direction – toward the preservation of the system.

Surely this criticism is so devastating that only a fool would support such a hypothesis? The question is whether anyone ever has, or rather, even if someone has been silly enough to do so, whether pluralist theory is logically committed to the hypothesis that power is not merely relatively widely diffused but that any actor who wishes to be active may, through political organization, influence decision-making. It appears on surface inspection that this is so. Several critiques of pluralism produce as the decisive proof a sentence from the most rigorous pluralist theorist of the lot – R. A. Dahl. The sentence is: 'A central guiding thread of American constitutional development has been the evolution of a political system in which all the active and legitimate groups in the population can make themselves heard at some crucial stage in the process of decision' (*A Preface to Democratic Theory* (1956), p. 137). That sentence is quoted in part by a number of critics – notably Miliband (*The State*, p. 4), Carole Pateman (*Participation and Democratic Theory* (1970), p. 15) and in a neglected but intelligent and respectful criticism by Shin'ya Ono ('The Limits of Bourgeois Pluralism', *Studies on the Left* (1965), p. 61).

The part quoted is that beginning with 'all . . .'. Even the whole sentence makes clear that this is not a description of a state of affairs but an aspiration in a process of political development. Dahl could argue in 1956 that US democratic practices *do* work in this direction, if haltingly and often slowly. He could point to the gradual destruction of white hegemony over blacks in the South, the entry of blacks into political participation through voting, party membership and civil rights struggles. If one reads the whole book then it is obvious that the sentence is not merely radically qualified but that its whole meaning is changed. In *A Preface to Democratic Theory* Dahl makes it abundantly clear that 'all active and legitimate groups' does *not* mean that *all* the citizens are included in the political process. Dahl makes it evident and emphasizes the fact that many citizens are inactive, that income and wealth and political resources are unequally distributed. Active groups thus cover a subset of US citizens. Legitimate groups exclude or have excluded communists and blacks in the South; Dahl makes clear the force and unlawful practices necessary to silence the blacks in the post-Reconstruction period. He does this consistently, but, embarrasingly for our quoting critics, on p. 138 in the paragraph immediately following the one so widely quoted. Dahl also makes clear that even if a policy is supported by the vast mass of the citizens *and* the Legislature it may not become law or lead to executive action – he illustrates this by over twenty years of resistance to legislation regulating child labour by the Supreme Court.

Dahl was writing of a country where a large minority were fighting for basic civil rights and others were oppressed by Draconian laws, in the full consciousness of those facts and evidently without approving of them. Yet he concluded that the US was a polyarchical political system and possessed of a sufficient degree of pluralism to qualify as such. Polyarchy is a matter of degree. This is the point ignored by most critics: that pluralist theory can generate a number of hypotheses and can lead to very different descriptions of political systems. We will return to this point when we outline and reconsider Dahl's theory; for the moment we must remain with the critics.

Dahl is clearly puzzled by the misreadings of his critics and in *Dilemmas of Pluralist Democracies* (1982), Appendix A, notes with some regret their selective use of sentences from *Who Governs?* (1961) and *A Preface to Democratic Theory*. Dahl's theory specifies 'polyarchy' as the relatively open competition of political elites by means of periodic electoral contests and in a political system in which there is a plurality of political forces, organizations and forms of influence over decision-making. The concept of polyarchy works through a multi-dimensional set of scales and included in these scales are the conditions for minimal democratic competition. Dahl demonstrates that the maximum conditions for democracy are virtually unrealizable and that most systems operate at much lower levels of inclusiveness and openness. The scales, however, provide a standard of measure of the degree of democratic competition. The theory provides the possibility that a Western industrial country will fail to meet the minimum conditions of public contestation and inclusiveness of participation in elections and the struggle for office. It would then be, in Dahl's terms, either a competitive oligarchy, if it failed on the scale of inclusiveness, or a closed or inclusive hegemony, if it failed on the scale of contestation. Hence a variety of descriptions are open to Dahl – there is no reason why, by virtue of the theory, the USA, for example, should fall under one rather than another. It is a matter of measurement and concrete analysis. But the critics are saying that Dahl and the other pluralists are more than empirically wrong; they are arguing that the very framework is flawed and must lead to such empirical 'errors', furthermore, that in doing so it legitimates the principal forms of domination in the West.

It would appear then, that pluralist theory cannot be an effective tool of criticism of Western polities and cannot find them radically wanting. Dahl's later work simply refutes this assertion and it remains consistent with the theoretical framework outlined earlier in *A Preface to Democratic Theory*. Before considering that, it is worthwhile examining why the critics could be so confident of the inherent ideological limitations of pluralism and what was at stake for them ideologically in their critique. Actually pluralist theory *has* generally functioned as an apologia for Western democracy. It has seldom been used as a tool of criticism, showing how close many of those polities have come to breaking the minimum conditions for effective political competition and to lacking a sufficient degree of inclusiveness of citizens and organizations to count as full polyarchies. Pluralism was used, along with the concept of 'totalitarianism' as its negative foil, to show the West as inherently democratic and the socialist East as barbarically authoritarian. The Congress-for-Cultural-Freedom view of the world is too well known to need repeating nor do its hireling or client intellectuals need naming.[2] A superficial observer might regard pluralism as *Encounter*'s house brand of political theory. But the potential of a theory is never exhausted by its least intelligent or most mendacious exponents. This would be equivalent to damning evolutionary theories in biology by mentioning only Lamarck, Oken and Erasmus Darwin and ignoring Charles Darwin. Why did the left critics fail to turn pluralism against the apologists and use it to show the extent to which the West stood in need of radical political reforms to make democracy work? Virtually none of the critics of pluralism were apologists for 'actually existing socialism' and almost all of them were committed to a society in which there was more not less democratic control. I will divide the critics loosely in two groups, the Marxists and the radicals.

The Marxist critics by no means form a 'school'. Ralph Miliband and Nicos Poulantzas held diametrically opposite views on the nature of the capitalist state and the manner in which the ruling class exercised domination, but both agreed that it did so and that pluralism was an erroneous and ideological view of political power under capitalism. Miliband, in *The State in Capitalist Society*, argued that pluralism was empirically wrong, that the personnel of the ruling class controlled the key decisions and that the influence of the subordinate classes was minimal on any matter affecting the basic economic and political relations of capitalism. Further, he argued that through ideology and through its control of education and the mass media, the ruling class was able to make its view prevail on a significant proportion of the subordinate classes. Miliband found pluralism wrong in its account of the first dimension of power and lacking in any cognizance of the second. For Poulantzas, both in his review of Miliband and in *Political Power and Social Classes* (1973), the third dimension was primary. Irrespective of the actual personal wealth, educational background or subjective outlook of the personnel of the ruling class, they are constrained to act in a certain way by the structural role of the capitalist state. Göran Therborn, 'What Does the Ruling Class Do when it Rules?', in A. Giddens and D. Held (eds), *Classes, Power and Conflict* (1982) likewise adopted this structural conception, rejecting other views – and including Miliband along with the pluralists – as part of the 'subjectivist approach'. Dahl had argued that political contestation in polyarchical societies was possible and containable because of a norma- tive consensus underlying conflict and which represented a tolerance of or active commitment to the replacement of one elite by another as a result of elections and the contest by groups to influence decision- making. Therborn asks: 'But what if "consensus" is the surface man- ifestation of something else, "enveloping, restricting and conditioning" electoral politics?' ('What Does the Ruling Class Do?', p. 231). Dahl treats conflict as a surface phenomenon made possible by consensus. Therborn treats consensus as a surface manifestation of the underlying structures of capitalist society.

Therborn's question shows just how question-begging is the whole reference to the 'third dimension'. Dahl, in *Polyarchy* (1971), analyses the conditions for consensus, drawing on definite objective conditions – such as level of socio-economic development, the degree of socio- economic inequality and perceptions of and responses to it, the degree to which the means of violence and socio-economic sanction are concentrated or dispersed, the pattern of sub-cultural and group rela- tions, and the beliefs of political activists as formed by political experience and political culture. Dahl is quite clear about and also specifies the conditions under which such a consensus is not formed or breaks down. The trouble with the Marxist variant of the 'third dimension' is that domination becomes an inherent and unequivocal attribute of a certain type of social structure. Dahl makes clear that consensus *is* the manifestation of something else – a relatively pluralistic social structure and one with integrative relationships sufficiently strong that social cleavages are not destructive of inter-group relations. But the 'third-dimensional' argument as used by Marxists does not have this degree of specificity. It leads to one of two conclusions: either that a pluralist consensus is the product of a politics attuned to the stable dominance of the capitalist ruling class, but this consensus is threatened by the objective contradictions of the capitalist system, or, that capitalism has so dominated and manipulated the imagination, needs and expectations of the subordinate classes that its rule is virtually unchallengeable. No one to my knowledge has ever carried the full logic of the 'third dimension' to the latter conclusion, not even Marcuse in the worst excesses of pessimism about one-dimensional man.

The former conclusion is no less shaky in that it rests on the assumption that there is a built-in series of contradictions which will break down the consensus and that the *real* entry of the working classes into politics will shatter the pluralist system. This proposition has no difficulty in appearing plausible until, that is, one asks just what is required for this event to happen? Gross inequality, mass unemployment, poor housing, bad working and living conditions? But these conditions faced the working class of Europe and America at the end of the nineteenth century and still face large sections of workers even in the most affluent capitalist countries like the USA today. At the end of the nineteenth century the 'working classes' in Europe did enter into politics and used the system of polyarchy to campaign to broaden the franchise where necessary, to create political parties and trade unions, and to press for and to achieve significant social reforms. Dahl's *Polyarchy* stresses this as one of the historical achievements of and also a demonstration of the truth of polyarchy. He also points out that nowhere have political organizations managed to organize the *whole* 'working class' and to create a situation of polarized political contestation where it confronts the 'bourgeoisie'. Dahl argues both that there are other patterns of cleavage than worker versus capitalist – ethnic, linguistic, regional, occupational, etc. – and that the wealthy and business groups are likewise divided. Confronting the evidence for massive inequalities in income and wealth in the USA, in a later work, Dahl concludes: 'Sometimes findings like these are thought to demonstrate the existence of a ruling class, they do not. What they demonstrate is the existence of great inequality in the distribution of economic resources; and insofar as economic resources are convertible to political resources, the figures also demonstrate severe inequality in the distribution of political resources' (*Dilemmas*, p. 173).

Ultimately the whole Marxist version of the 'third-dimension' argument reduces to two propositions: first, genuine socialist alternatives are nowhere effectively presented to the electorate, chosen and put into effect; second, the reason for this is the effective control both of the political agenda and the means of violence and socio-economic sanction by the ruling class.

If socialist alternatives are presented and rejected by the electorate the reason is ideological hegemony. If socialist parties are elected to government they cannot pose a real threat of an alternative to capitalism or if they do they are subordinated through the pressure of the state machine. The crucial role in sustaining capitalism here is ultimately given to ideology. The very idea that socialist alternatives *are* regularly presented to the electorate and turned down is impossible to accept as such. Clearly complex factors must intervene to overdetermine the people's choice. Thus the dismal electoral failure of the British Communist Party (which has regularly stood in elections, goes out of its way to appear both radical and reasonable, and has regularly lost several hundred deposits and won no parliamentary seats) needs explaining. Perhaps ordinary people are not clever enough to find the actually existing socialism of the USSR massively unattractive and the alternative ideas of a democratic non-authoritarian socialism vague and unconvincing? Revolutionary socialism has been a widely known alternative for over a hundred years, during which time several advanced capitalist countries have had broadly based electorates (if not full adult suffrage) and has never been chosen by more than a politically containable minority.

Here the pluralist argument finds Marxist theory and revolutionary socialist practice at the two points of greatest weakness. One has already been stated – the failure of the socialist left to win in relatively open electoral competition, with universal adult suffrage and a secret ballot. For example, the British Communist Party is allowed the occasional party political broadcast during general elections and you can buy a cheap daily newspaper called *The Morning Star* if you really want one. The other failure is more galling, since we can blame the former on Rupert Murdoch and those Oxbridge-educated BBC types. The Marxist account of the democratic alternative to capitalism – popular participatory commune democracy, as outlined in Marx's *Civil War in France* (1871) – has nowhere proved possible to institute in a socialist country and there are good theoretical reasons for believing it to be utopian. Such a direct democracy is defeated by the size of the population and the complexity of the tasks in a medium-sized, advanced industrial country and a smaller country would be unable to defend itself against external predators. The Paris Commune of 1871 illustrates the problem.

Its internal affairs were virtual chaos, and it was administering what was in modern terms no more than one medium-sized city. Furthermore, the Commune was not *that* radical or socialist in its policy, and would have lost even more support if it had been. We shall have reason to return to the Commune's appalling end, to the butchery carried out by Thiers's supporters.

Galling in the extreme is the absence of the 'alternative' and the existence of at least some moderately successful forms of polyarchy. They are, as even their intelligent proponents accept, at best a minimalist form of democracy. They do, however, 'work' on the large scale of a complex industrial society and do deliver the little they claim to do – some influence over decisions and some political freedoms for the ordinary people who have the time, money and energy to use them. Moreover, authoritarian socialism does exist too and is so actively disliked by most ordinary people that if they have a choice between it and a minimalist form of democracy they overwhelmingly choose the latter. The Marxists and revolutionary socialists are arguing for an absent and probably utopian 'alternative'. Hence their need to deny the reality of minimalist democracy, to show it as domination. But what is the acid test of that domination? Why, the capacity to remove the 'alternative' from the political agenda!

Let us return to the question of the ruling class. Dahl accepts 'severe inequality in the distribution of political resources' as a possibility and, as we shall see, accepts that corporate business has an altogether unwarranted share of economic activity and political influence in America, if that country is to be more than a very minimalist version of polyarchy indeed. Let us then suppose that in the United States the major corporations' executives, senior government officials, Members of Congress and senior politicians, and wealthy and influential 'notables' in localities each form part of the ruling class, but that small businesspeople and medium-sized capitalist employers of labour, big farmers and the top 5 per cent of income earners do not, forming, rather, a supporting social base and a recruitment stratum for ruling class personnel. Even so we are faced in the USA with a large number of people – several tens of thousands at a minimum, drawn from and communicating with a stratum numbering millions. Even if we ignore ethnic and regional interests, or even occupational and business-sector interests, there is more than enough scope for the narrower stratum to develop very divergent positions, groupings or factions, and to need to enter into organized relations of contestation within itself. In other words, even if we ignore the vast majority of the population and ignore even the support base of the ruling class, that class will not be homogeneous in interests or policies. Any intelligent version of the theory of the ruling class or power elite must accept that even in a

medium-sized industrial country its members will form a large number
and will be in need of political mechanisms for coping with that fact.
Even if we were to suppose that the vast mass of the population lacked
political rights this would remain so – oligarchic contestation also
requires specific political forms and interest organizations. Our 'ruling
class' is already a small and politically divided republic bigger than most
of those of the Ancients or Renaissance Italy. Most versions of Marxism
accept that the ruling class is divided into 'fractions' and that different
parts of the state apparatus have different views and interests.

Once we introduce the fact that the adult population does have
political rights and that a significant minority, but much larger than the
'ruling class' or its support stratum, makes active use of them, then we
must think again. For the contestation between ruling class factions now
extends out to mobilizing the support in elections and other forms of
political participation of the portions of that active part of the adult
population perceived to be closest to them in interests and outlook.
Elite/ruling class contestation finds reflection in parties and elections.
Even if we assume no party or organization is active which is *not*
sponsored by some ruling-class faction – that there is no independent
organized labour party; everyone is born 'a little Liberal or else a little
Conservative' – some surprising things start to happen. First, competing
factions must bid for support and, therefore, 'buy' votes and influence;
this means attending to non-ruling-class interests. Second, the 'ruling-
class' factions must constantly co-opt the most active and effective of the
non-members or lose their capacity to relate to subordinate strata.
Already one is beginning to see channels of reciprocal influence
developing as a result of the widening of the political contestation to
involve getting the support of subordinate strata.

We have assumed a political contest wholly dominated by ruling class
factions and even then – assuming minimal democracy, that is, elections
plus civil rights – we reach some measure of influence by the subordinate
strata. Only a factionless 'ruling class' could escape this logic, but then it
would have to be quite small, hundreds or a few thousands of notables,
and very homogeneous. Such a concentrated 'closed hegemony' (a
concept developed in *Polyarchy*) is typical of a relatively backward
agrarian society where landownership is highly concentrated and where
subordinate strata are enmeshed in paternalistic or clientelage relations
of direct dependence on the large landowners. Even then it is a bit too
ideal–typical for its own good. Any concept of 'ruling class' incompatible with the claim that power and influence are relatively widely diffused
in an advanced industrial capitalist polity would have to ignore basic
aspects of its economic, social and political structure. But that surely
would be in contradiction with the main explanatory principle of
Marxism?

In practice Marxists do allow for political competition within the ruling class and its reflection in the political processes of the wider society. But they lack a rigorous theoretical account of why the ruling class is divided and how this affects its 'rule'. Such an account is provided by pluralism and the concept of polyarchy. Indeed, pluralism provides a theoretical framework which can accommodate both considerable inequality based on socio-economic inequality, and a significant measure of the diffusion of power and influence. It also provides indicators of possible forms of reform that would reduce inequality and would permit the enhanced influence and power of non-wealthy strata. An intelligent Marxist would have to argue in order to sustain any sort of criticism that pluralism does not wholly explain the workings of the political system, and that the state in particular is a continuous organization and one whose personnel are less accessible to the influence of forces other than the well-organized and powerful. An intelligent pluralist might reply to this criticism, 'perhaps not but then it doesn't have to.' Pluralism is a theory of democratic political competition and its conditions, and not an account of all social and political phenomena. The pluralist would be unwise to ignore the 'state' as a continuous and relatively closed organization with specialist personnel with ideas and interests of their own. But to the degree that that is true, so would the Marxist, for he or she too has much to learn from their own lesson.

Of the radical critics less need be said. By and large radical views of the limitations of pluralist accounts of power are based on the view that the wide diffusion of power is desirable and can be attained by democratic reforms. Radical 'two-dimensional' views of power seek to break the illegitimate control of powerful groups over the political agenda and are thus, in effect, arguing for a version of pluralism whilst denying its accuracy as an empirical account of the current distribution of power. Several radical critics of pluralism and polyarchical democracy are also arguing for the relevance of other forms of democratic organization and control. A good example is Pateman (*Participation*) who argues the relevance of the tradition of participatory and direct democracy.[3]

Curiously enough, Dahl – although one of the principal architects of the polyarchical theory – is also an exponent of participatory democracy. In a series of works (notably *After the Revolution?* (1970), *Dilemmas* and *A Preface to Economic Democracy* (1985)) he has argued for the appropriateness of participatory democracy in smaller local authorities and for the self-management of cooperatively owned economic enterprises. Dahl is usually criticized as if he argued that polyarchical elective democracy and the competition of organized elites were the only possible mechanisms of democratic influence and control. It is important to see why Dahl developed the concept of polyarchy. Dahl's argument both in *A Preface to Democratic Theory* and in *After the Revolution?*, where he answers radical democratic critics and takes up the issues of the students' movement, is that political mechanisms must be adjusted to the scale and complexity of the tasks involved. No one political mechanism can perform all the tasks of administration and decision-making. The limits of direct participatory democracy set in at a relatively low level of size (a few thousand) and at a relatively low level of complexity of the tasks of administration. Political authority cannot be scaled down in size to meet these limits if we want both to retain the benefit of large scale industry and also to deal with the problems it creates, like economic regulation, the control of pollution, the provision of community services, etc.

Dahl is, however, interested in how to preserve some measure of democracy – that is, a controlling influence by the demos – in large-scale political organization. He is thus quite unlike Max Weber who treats representative democracy as the plebiscitarian selection and legitimation of leaders, who then dominate the masses with an authoritarian power of command. Representative democracy for Dahl has several functions; it must confer political influence on the demos, it must ensure the political stability of the system, and it must prevent the demagogic manipulation of majorities in order to dominate minorities. This involves the difficult operation of steering between the Scylla of Weber's plebiscitarian leader-democracy and the Charybdis of de Tocqueville's tyranny of the majority. How is this actually accomplished in Western industrial societies? Certainly not by any radical innovation in democratic doctrine. Dahl makes clear that Western democratic theories and the constitutional arrangements of many states, such as the USA, were established long before the problems of large-scale complex industrial societies presented themselves.

Dahl finds the answer for polyarchical democracy in the pluralistic structure of such societies. He argues that a diversity of occupational, social, religious, ethnic and regional groups provides the foundation for effective 'secondary associations' and argues that these associations form the bedrock of the pluralistic competition for influence over decision-making that makes polyarchy possible. Two key conditions attach to this pluralism: first, that sub-cultural and group relations are not so fragmented and antagonistic as to undermine the consensus necessary to stable political competition, and second, that political authority is not so concentrated and closed as to prohibit effective political competition. A closed oligarchy will fear the consequences for itself of permitting open competition. Dahl argues that under advanced industrial conditions polyarchy may not exist if sub-cultural pluralism leads to antagonistic competition between groups or if the economic enterprises are dominated by a single central authority. This does *not* mean that Dahl sees capitalism as a precondition for pluralist democracy: 'The amount of organisational pluralism in a country does not appear to depend on whether enterprises are privately or socially owned. It does depend on the extent to which decisions are decentralised, that is, on the amount of autonomy permitted to enterprises' (Dahl, *Dilemmas*, p. 114). Dahl argues vigorously in *A Preface to Economic Democracy* that the concentration of economic ownership in large organizations, like business corporations, radically weakens democracy and pluralism. A considerable measure of economic autonomy for individual social agents is the precondition for their capacity to exert political influence. Extreme inequalities of income and wealth, and the concentration of economic power in large hierarchically managed corporations, reduces the pluralist social base of polyarchical democracy. Such inequality and concentration may, indeed, if we extend Dahl's argument in a more pessimistic direction than he does, cripple democracy.

Dahl argues in *Dilemmas*, therefore, that a reduction in economic concentration, the greater self-management of economic enterprises, the greater re-distribution of income and wealth, and the development of a welfare state are remedies for maintaining the health of American democracy. He also argues that American interest organizations are both decentralized and relatively exclusive; they are thus able to bargain and to influence decisions for their own members whilst leaving large sections of the population unorganized and at the mercy of the costs passed on as a consequence of these organizations' decisions. Dahl thus accepts with a measure of approval stable, highly inclusive and centralized corporatist representation and bargaining such as one finds in Sweden. Corporatism can thus be part of the pluralist account of political competition, and not a restriction of it as some commentators seem to think.

Polyarchy is a system in which a plurality of organizations compete for influence and specifically where formally equal electors have a choice between a number of parties in elections. It leads not to 'majority rule' but to minori*ties* rule: such a polity does not consist of an amorphous citizenry who cast their votes directly for policies, but of a highly differentiated body of supporters of secondary organizations, who cast their votes for parties related to those organisations. Votes thus shift to a limited degree between different parties and interests. 'Majorities' are made up of coalitions of minorities, either in the form of explicit bargaining between parties, or by the shift of votes toward one major party, which is itself an overarching coalition of interests. Interest organizations are themselves headed by elites and these elites are supported and influenced by circles of activists. Dahl accepts that large

interest organizations are complex bodies that are not immediately
responsive to their memberships, that they too involve processes of
representation, and that they are headed by elites. He argues, however,
that oligarchy in organizations is counteracted by the mutual competition of overlapping organizations for members. Competing organizations pose mutual threats to the possibility of their exclusive control of
members. Dahl concludes 'that the law of oligarchy bends more easily
than iron' (*Dilemmas*, p. 33).

Polyarchy avoids de Tocqueville's dilemma of majority tyranny
because the 'people' never are an equal and amorphous citizen body;
rather, the populace is structured into mutually conditioning interests
and organizations. Polyarchy avoids Weber's authoritarian plebiscitar-
ianism because of political competition between a plurality of organized
interests and parties; individual votes in organisational and national
elections may count for little but in aggregate they do count and voters
can be organized to replace one party or leadership by another and to
influence one policy rather than another. The demos, because it is
organized and organizable, and is represented through competing
parties, does have a limited but real influence. Hence polyarchy is not
merely a form of legitimation of rule; rather it is a form of remote and
limited but nevertheless real influence of the demos on decisions.

Dahl's theory is essentially an account of the minimum conditions for
effective political competition and the purpose of that competition is a
minimum level of influence of the demos on policy-making. Dahl makes
it clear that the model of polyarchy (see *Preface to Democratic Theory*,
Appendix to chapter 3, pp. 84–9) is a maximum specification of
democratic control and that on each of its eight component propositions
there are differential degrees of approach to the maximum. A polyarchy
is any organization in which all eight conditions scale at probabilities of
0.5. Thus a large number of regimes may score less on certain elements
of the model and yet remain closer to the polyarchical than to the
hegemonic or oligarchical corners of the matrix space onto which
regimes can be plotted, measured and classified. It is precisely this
complex and gradated space of evaluation which Marxism has lacked.
Its evaluations have been crude and dichotomistic, no less so than the
vulgar liberal opposition of democracy and totalitarianism.

As a theory of political competition Dahl's model is capable of
generating a number of variants and a wide range of descriptions of
political systems. Four main forms of competition are possible in terms
of the model, each with different consequences for the influence of
citizens on decisions. The first is the example of a polyarchy which meets
the minimum conditions: here is a political contest in which all active
and legitimate groups (not all groups or all citizens) can make themselves heard at some crucial stage in the process of decision, and over

time, if they are large enough and active enough, they will receive some measure of acceptance of or accommodation to their interests in decision-making that will suffice to keep them in the contest. The second is the example of a formally elective democracy in which competition takes place between mutually exclusive and antagonistic organized groups: here is a political contest in which at least one of the groups which prevails at a given time will seek to dominate the process of decision-making, exclude other groups from it, and will deny those groups accommodation in decision-making if that is possible. Here the norms of toleration of the elective circulation of elites and of the legitimacy of other groups pressing their claims are weak among at least some groups. If these norms are rejected by all groups, or if a group denying them gains power, a polyarchical system will probably be replaced by the hegemony of one group over others. We may call this 'antagonistic pluralism' rather than polyarchy, and good examples of it are the Weimar Republic after 1928 and the Lebanon today. A third form of political competition is different from the above, in that a regime is based upon a single party and even if there are elections they amount to no more than compulsory plebiscites which acclaim the pre-selected candidates of the party. This is a clear form of election-as-legitimation where authority is 'formally derived from the will of the governed' (Weber, *Economy and Society*, vol. 1, p. 268). This corresponds to what Dahl calls an 'inclusive hegemony'. In this system there is very little public contestation but the citizens have formal political rights to participate in elections. Two forms of competition will take place here: one is the contest of bureaucratic elites within the regime and of factions within the ruling party; this may serve to express differences in policy lines and to reflect popular attitudes and grievances, at least as they are channelled through officials and party members. The other is the regime's effort to ensure a decent turn-out in the plebiscite; this will offer some measure of popular influence if elections are not absolutely compulsory and not rigged by the secret police. The fourth form of competition is what Dahl, in *Polyarchy*, calls a 'competitive oligarchy'. Here elite groups compete for and share power, drawing their votes and support from a narrow and exclusive section of the population. An example would be the British Parliamentary system before the 1832 Reform Act. Dahl argues that where such competition has been institutionalized and the norms of competing for and ceding power are accepted, then the democratization of such a system in the direction of greater inclusiveness has a high probability of leading to a stable polyarchy. Stable polyarchy is not the only form of political competition nor the only form of mass political influence therefore. It is not difficult to see the advantages of polyarchy over forms two and three, or the need to reform the fourth, if one subscribes even in a qualified way to democratic values. However, polyarchy is not something that can be 'chosen' irrespective of social structural conditions: it would be difficult to sustain in a centralized bureaucratically controlled economy of an advanced industrial country or in a relatively poor Third World country with gross inequalities in access to wealth, education and communications, even if the members of the significant elites are committed to the requisite democratic values.

Polyarchy can also be threatened or radically degraded below the minimum level of performance even in an advanced industrial country without a centralized economy and with widespread and at least formal support for the requisite democratic values. Dahl himself provides an account of why this is so. Extreme inequality in incomes, combined with exclusive and decentralized interest organizations and bargaining processes, will leave many sections of society who badly need representing without effective organizational spokesmen. A large section of the population may be economically and politically marginalized. Under-participation in organizations and elections may radically reduce the proportion of the population in the 'active and legitimate' category of citizens. Either the needs and preferences of many citizens go unexpressed or those citizens who are ignored by the political process turn to means that are less than legitimate. Such inequality of influence and participation is characteristic of the contemporary United States. A very low percentage of the US workforce (20 per cent) is organized in trade unions. A very high percentage of the US electorate fails to vote, even in Presidential elections (where 40 per cent abstention is the norm). Neither of these facts is important in itself – for example, a higher turnout may not radically alter outcomes in elections – nor are they recent phenomena. Many pluralists have cautioned against the 'over-participation' of the masses in politics, but Dahl's model of polyarchy shows under-participation in certain specific circumstances to be an equal danger.

The system of 'minorities rule' can stop recruiting citizens at some point well up on the pyramid of income and wealth. Economic inequality is then converted into structured political inequality. As Dahl realizes, this must lead to a highly restricted political agenda: 'The unequal resources that allow organisations to stabilise injustice also enable them to exercise unequal influence in determining what alternatives are seriously considered' (*Dilemmas*, p. 47). Politics becomes a matter of relatively narrow and well-organized interest groups competing for immediate benefits for themselves, to the exclusion of 'alternatives that promise substantial long-run benefits to a larger number of unorganised citizens' (ibid.). Dahl is thus quite capable of operating in his own version of intent Lukes calls the third dimension, although his is one very different from that of the Marxists.

The result of marginalization and under-participation, on the one hand, and the concentration of organizations into competing issue-groups representing relatively narrow interests, on the other, is to damage radically the values on which polyarchical democracy depends. A large proportion of the population becomes apathetic, cynical or despairing about the political process and the value of participation. Sections of the politically active portion adopt an increasingly instrumental and interest-centred attitude toward the political process and are only interested in certain outcomes. The result is an increasingly restricted and negative 'civic culture', in which the common good or the rights of other groups cease to be a focus of common concern. Many Americans, including pluralist theorists, are worried that these processes are accelerating in the United States and that they are finding very clear reflection in the two mainstream political parties. The Democrats are held by many commentators to have declined into a loose coalition of interest groups and the Republicans organize as a party on a very narrow social base and one which puts its own immediate interests stridently to the fore.

When one couples this development with the concentration of corporate power in the United States economy, recognizing clearly the unaccountable character of managerial control, and one allows for the vested interests built-into the huge Federal government machine, then the scope for restricting the political agenda is further reinforced. Dahl continues to believe that the United States not only has to take action to reduce economic and political inequality but that it will do so, in some late-twentieth-century version of the New Deal which makes America more like Sweden. Perhaps so. But if the trends Dahl and others identify continue, then the USA could soon be in the semi-polyarchy class, and, despite formal rights to vote and participate, the *de facto* absence of a large portion of the citizens from the political process could lead to its resembling Dahl's category of competitive oligarchy. Pluralism is capable of generating a number of different descriptions of and hypotheses about power in advanced industrial societies. Not all of them are as comforting as the conventional wisdom of the 1950s. Dahl's example should show, however, that pluralist theory has a rigour and complexity hardly suspected by its critics.

One thing pluralism tells us very little about is the state. The political process in a polyarchy is treated as a medium of contestation and the governmental process is treated as broadly responsive to the successful parties and organizations in that contestation. There is a great deal of truth in this: governments do change and so do policies, lobbying interests are accommodated, and protesting citizens may be heeded. But the state is a continuing organization, an assemblage of organizations and institutions with permanent officials, with continuing policies and 'departmental views'. Big government is now so big that those policies and views cannot be either coherent across the whole range of government activity or wholly controlled by the formally responsible political leaders. This can be accommodated in part by corporate bargaining, selective lobbying and public protest. Certainly the problem is more manageable in a relatively open polyarchy with active secondary associations than in any other political system. Nevertheless, the process of minorit*ies* rule and complex bargaining combined with the complex and multi-faced nature of big government means that large-scale policies of a radical nature, requiring coordination between different departments and proceeding in opposition to entrenched and effectively organized interests, will encounter great difficulty and will be, at best, only partly implemented. This is partly because of the 'drag' imposed by big government and partly because of the effects of minorit*ies* rule, which deny to radical political leaders the level of support and the time in government to be effective in the implementation of major policies. All this is exacerbated in a system like that of the United States, where the executive and the legislature may be of very different political complexions. Pluralism and big government together mean that radical reforms require more support than governments normally get and a long period in office. Sweden is exceptional in the degree of support for the Social Democratic governments and their long period of uninterrupted office in the post-1945 period. A measure of popular support greater than that mobilized for the New Deal would be required if the measures proposed by Dahl, more radical than those of the 1930s, were to be acceptable. Political marginalization and under-participation means that that support is unlikely to be forthcoming.

A pluralist analysis can thus lead to some highly pessimistic conclusions about the prospects for radical political change by means of the normal processes of polyarchy, especially when it is supplemented by an account of the nature of continuing big government. This also applies to other radical views of fundamental structural reforms. Not only do these facts undermine Dahl's own radical agenda but to a degree those of radical democratic socialists in most of the countries of Western Europe. Far from revelling in the facts of economic and political inequality, of under-participation and political marginalization, the restriction of the agenda, and the 'drag' imposed by big government on radical reforms, because they can be used as a challenge to the pluralist thesis that power is relatively widely diffused in Western democracies, Marxists and radicals might reflect on the implications of these facts for their own practices and aspirations.

To the extent that power does remain relatively widely diffused in Western democracies, that fact confers a legitimacy on these political systems by comparison with polities like the USSR and, therefore, weakens the appeal of 'actually existing socialism' beyond vanishing point. To the extent that economic and political inequality lead to the *de facto* exclusion and demoralization of a substantial portion of the population, and that exclusion is combined with a working system of minori*ties* rule, then together these circumstances weaken the political base for radical reformist strategies. Instead of worrying about a 'ruling class' which would destroy radical attempts at change, as the Marxist critics of pluralism tend to do, or arguing that ideology restricts the political agenda so that it never happens that a radical attempt becomes feasible, we would be better employed using pluralist theory in combination with Marxism to explain the structurally weak place of radical and democratic socialist alternatives in such a political system.

I have said nothing of revolutionary seizures of power because under contemporary Western conditions they are simply an absurd fantasy. Modern states have that monopoly of the means of violence and a degree of effective organization which can reliably suppress even large and determined groups of people with nothing to lose and the support of the majority of the population. In Western countries, there will always be a determined minority who make the action of the forces of repression socially sustainable. If, as I said earlier, even a restrictive definition of the 'ruling class' includes a large number of persons and its support stratum a much larger number, and in a medium-sized industrial country like the UK that combined number is in the millions, then one can see why the forces of 'order' will be supported and sustained. Unless that ruling class and support stratum is so divided and polarized as to draw upon factions in the subordinate population in order to pursue its quarrels by violent rather than polyarchical means, and unless that quarrel divides and disorganizes the state's monopoly of the means of violence, then 'revolution' cannot occur. This is not an 'elitist' challenge to Marxism, it is a point repeatedly stressed by Lenin and codified in such orthodox Third International political manuals as *Armed Insurrection*. It is also a point realized by Marx and Engels, and one of the reasons why they supported and encouraged the competition of the SPD in elections for the *Reichstag*. The Commune of 1871 perished not merely because it was made in a single city but because within that city and as refugees from it were not only the *grande bourgeoisie* and the *rentiers*, but also a mass of hostile petty bourgeois. It was they and their fear which stoked the bloodlust of Thiers's troops and led to days of continuing and merciless vengeance.

When Bernstein pointed out, in *Evolutionary Socialism* (1899), the ruling class was composed of a large number and its support stratum an even larger one – taking both categories from orthodox Marxism – he was saying nothing new; nor did he say anything exceptional when he argued they formed a veto group against undemocratic social change and thus committed the socialist movement to fighting by filling the ballot boxes. What *did* upset the orthodox was his claim that, far from getting smaller, that section of the population would remain, and his claim that the workers would not come to enjoy the sort of sociological majority necessary for the sort of electoral majority required for the legitimation of revolutionary social change. If we remove our hitherto simplistic assumptions about social topography, no longer assuming that agents act in conformity with their place in the social relations of production or even their actual occupational position, then the social homogeneity of the subordinate strata and their potential aggregation and mobilization into a political majority vanish too.

Marxism itself raises the problem of theorizing pluralism once we remove the optimistic and incorrect assumption that the long-term processes of modern capitalistic economies create a relatively homogeneous and majority 'working class'. Remove that assumption and accept that the 'ruling class' forms a large number, and then the need, within Marxism, for a theory like pluralism becomes evident. It is a pity that Marxists have spent so long decrying and systematically misunderstanding promising and rigorous theories like those of R. A. Dahl.[4] It is all the more a pity when the theorist in question, far from being a died-in-the-wool reactionary, is far to the left of the American political spectrum.

I have left one name out of this account so far, Tom Bottomore. He has always stood for a humane democratic socialism and a Marxism open and able to renew itself from non-Marxist thought whenever necessary. He has long championed the Austro-Marxists, pioneers in such a stance. I doubt he will agree with the whole of this chapter, but I hope he will see in it evidence of my having learned some lessons, even if it is long after they were taught to me.

4

The critical resources of established jurisprudence

(with Phil Jones)

Critical legal studies must reject the notion of 'critique' as its dominant intellectual principle. 'Critique' implies a double rejection of the criticized: firstly, a new critical theory uncontaminated by established jurisprudence that will facilitate a new practice in relation to law, and, secondly, the eventual emergence of an alternative set of institutions that has shed all the undesirable features of existing laws and legal forms. Attachment to the notion of critique arises in part from the desire for distinctiveness; to show the Critical Legal Studies movement to be decisively different from the ad hoc radical criticisms of law and different from the practice of giving established modes of legal theorizing and approaches to the study of law a radical twist. It implies a challenge to practitioners and academics who adopt a 'pink but expert' stance. All well and good, but the notion of 'critique' involves a real danger. That danger is the rejection, in the name of radicalism, of the genuine benefits entailed in Western liberal legal systems and in the forms of knowledge developed by legal theorists in the critical elaboration and defence of Western liberalism. By liberalism here we mean a primary concern with the freedom of the citizen and of associations freely formed by citizens.

'Critique' is a concept with a solid Marxist-Hegelian pedigree, but to adopt the stance of 'critique' one need subscribe neither to dialectical-materialist metaphysics nor to Frankfurt school critical theory. Aside from such specific theorizations, the notion of critique involves the supposition that contemporary reality contains within it an alternative, an emerging possibility that will supplant existing forms of social organization and one which is superior to them. The task of theory or critical knowledge is to discern that alternative, and to do so the critique must cast aside the forms of reasoning which are tied to the existing conditions and the ideas implicated in them. This rejection need not imply a Marxist politics, any more than it implies a Marxist theory: anarchists, radical feminists and radical ecologists all advance versions of the notion of 'critique'.

'Critique' would be a harmless game played by intellectuals, a thinking persons' equivalent of *Trivial Pursuits*, if it did not include one essential feature, that it is a challenge to existing institutions and ideas which rejects them wholesale. The essence of criticial theory, a theory which penetrates behind appearances and the given forms, is the existence of an 'alternative' – a concrete possibility radically different from the forms dominant in the present and contained as a successor to them within contemporary reality. Without the 'alternative', critique distintegrates and turns into criticism, and change becomes definite projects of reform rather than being the revolutionary essence present in reality itself, anticipating a future to be. The notion of an 'alternative' implies that what is supplanted has a characteristic form and a distinctive governing principle, that it can be replaced without admixture with that which supplants it and without loss. In the case of law the notion of an 'alternative' supposes that what is to be supplanted has an institutional form tied to the existing social arrangements and has a function only within such arrangements. Thus Marxism traditionally supposed that law was definitely tied to capitalist commodity production and to the class state, and that in the course of creating a communist society, distinctively legal forms of organization and regulation will wither away along with the state itself.

Few now support the more crass forms of the revolutionary Marxist approach to law and only a small number of people of whatever persuasion imagine that a radical alternative to law as we know it is a feasible objective for political struggle today. The danger in retaining the concept of 'critique' is not so much the conscious striving for an unattainable alternative, a utopia, but the unconscious retention of the habit of thinking in antinomian terms, as if the present legal forms and institutions were an entity that can be challenged in essence. The danger of the notion of 'critique', rather than criticism, is that it will unify law as the object of the critique and ascribe to law a single social function. If absurd revolutionary optimism is avoided, then the result of retaining the form of 'critique' is a pessimism that denies all aspects of the present any legitimacy, but cannot in practice supplant it. The revolutionary is replaced by the cultural critic.

As we have said, Marxism is not the only form of 'critique', but its failure is instructive and ought to sober those who seek some other 'alternative'. As a political theory Marxism claimed to supplant and render obsolete over 2,000 years of political and jurisprudential thinking about the state and law. Marxism rejected detailed thought about the contemporary institutional forms of either the state or law because both were destined to become obsolete and to be replaced without loss. Marxism is a failure as a political theory because it stakes all on an impossible alternative, an advanced society with modern industry but without either a separate public power or a formal legal framework. No one now seriously believes that the state will 'wither away'. Once the full extent of Marxism's failure in this matter of political theory is clear we should begin to undo its demolition job, its critique, of existing forms of political and legal theory. We cannot remain in that special variety of post-Marxist prison where Marxism offers no distinctive potential future and yet existing forms of thought and institutions are half-unconsciously rejected as 'liberal' or 'bourgeois'. Marx certainly would not have done so; the great objectivist would have faced circumstances and set to work repairing the damage. More than 2,000 years of theorizing and in-tellectual work have to be taken off the garbage heap and carefully sifted.

In particular we need to be specially careful about the last 200 years, the period when Marx and Marxists faced their contemporaries and near-contemporaries as political competitors and were ruthless in their usage of them as such. It is in that period that liberal political theory elaborated its doctrine and stated the social, political and legal condi-tions for the irreducible minimum of freedom of the citizen and of associations freely formed of citizens. In particular, it is necessary to re-evaluate attempts to refine and defend liberalism in the conjucture of the death of Marxism in Stalinism and the challenge of fascism. The most sophisticated legal theorists of Marxism in the 1930s, those who enjoyed the freedom to think, Karl Renner, Otto Kirchheimer and Franz Neumann all adopted variants of liberalism and representative democracy. To borrow a phrase from another and more sinister discourse, this is no accident.

We shall claim that at least four traditions in modern Western jurisprudence together provide the elements of an account of an advanced liberal-pluralist political and legal order. We shall claim that such an account is essential for the criticism and reform of the dominant forms of politics, that it is no apologia for existing conditions and a simple ideology which flings the 'freedom' of the West against the 'totalitarianism' of the East. On the contrary, we face a conjuncture where the advanced industrial societies of East and West both desper-ately need reform, a need recognized even by the leaders in the East and a need barely recognized by either leaders or populace in the West. If the USSR desperately needs liberal-pluralist reforms to drag it out of its post-Stalinist bureaucratico-sclerotic coma, the USA needs liberal-pluralist reforms to prevent it sinking into a state not far removed from a capitalist plutocracy.

The four traditions are:

1 the defence of the political autonomy of law as essential to democratic pluralism, advanced by Otto Kirchheimer and Franz Neumann;[1]
2 the defence of the primacy of the freedom of citizens and of the freedom of associations formed by citizens against the state by English 'pluralists' like J. N. Figgis and F. W. Maitland, using critically Otto von Gierke's theory of associations;[2]
3 H. L. A. Hart's defence of the 'internal view' in relation to the citizens of a legal order, an order which they accept and comprehend as legitimate;[3]
4 Carl Schmitt's authoritarian conservative exposure of the blindness and limits of classical liberalism, the need to recognize friend–enemy relations and the state of exception when formulating the rule of law.[4]

Others, less directly jurisprudential, could be added, such as the pluralist theory of political competition of R. A. Dahl, but an excursion outside the arena of legal theory is unnecessary here as Dahl has been discussed in chapter 3.

Western pluralism and liberalism (in the senses used above and *not* in the sense of the essentially economic liberalism of F. A. von Hayek) are a heritage we renounce at our peril. This is not to say there is nothing to criticize in the contemporary Western democracies that formally claim to be liberal and pluralistic. On the contrary, our theoretical heritage suitably exploited provides both the intellectual tools for criticism and value standards for justifying such criticism. What it does not sustain is the notion of 'critique'. On the contrary, within any intelligible future short of the complete ruin of Western societies and polities, liberal-pluralism demonstrates certain forms of organization and certain value standards which are unsurpassable, to which there is no 'alternative'.

LEGAL ORDER AND PLURALISM

Liberal pluralism makes the freedom of the citizens and associations freely chosen by citizens its primary value and main theoretical concern. But the very notion of a legal order implies a 'pluralism' of another sort: it is difficult to conceive of a legal order in a society without institutional differentiation and yet with a single and binding code of conduct. 'Law' yes, but not a legal order. A legal order is not primarily a code of sanctioned norms applied to the conduct of individuals. The Decalogue is 'law', in the sense of a set of rules governing conduct applied by authorities whose powers have become customary, but it does not as such give rise to a legal order. In this sense John Austin's[5] distinction between 'law' and 'positive morality' had value, even if it is unsustainable in his own theoretical terms. For Austin the difference turned on a determinate superior whose commands were habitually obeyed, but the essence of a legal order consists less in the determinateness of the superior than in the character of the agents regulated. A tribal chieftain is a 'sovereign' for Austin, if his status is that of an uncommanded commander. But the chief is not a separate public power; to twist Austin's terms he is merely an expression and executor of customary positive morality. A separate public power, regulating through a legal order, exists when its task of regulation is open ended and its role is independent of given customs or the opinions of a singular body of subordinates. The separate public power and independent legal order exist because they regulate a public sphere of institutional complexity: individuals who occupy multiple and distinct roles; institutions and associations with a distinct function and corporate life. Then, given this complex 'civil society', seperation, determinateness and primacy belong of necessity to the public power. It begins to resemble a 'sovereign' in Austin's sense, claiming to be the dominant source of binding rules and the society of societies, above the associations and the roles of its citizens. A legal order implies a differentiated public sphere. Society must be composed of associations and differentiated roles to require a 'sovereign'.

Law in the developed sense of a legal order implies three major elements.

1   The first is a realm of differentiated agencies of decision, a complex of independent decision-making agencies interacting in some definite area of activity and where conduct is not given or exhaustively prescribed. Such a realm requires regulation, and static custom alone will not suffice, but that regulation does not, as such, presuppose a single separate public power. It presupposes some arrangements acceptable to the agents – such as a representative council elected by them or an agreed arbitrator. Trade associations or cartels are examples of such regulation.[6]

2   As we have seen, the existence of just one realm of differentiated agencies of decision does not imply a legal order, merely some regulatory arrangements. It is the interaction of a number of distinct realms of such agencies that changes the picture. Such an interaction requires one overall instance of regulation, separate from and not reducible to any one area of activity or agent. The complex interactions of distinct realms and agents prohibit regulation by ad hoc negotiation between the representatives of the different realms. Therefore, such an instance of regulation must be both separate and compelling – a single public power. But it cannot be the ad hoc rule of Austin's 'sovereign': its power to make rules may or may not be unlimited in content but cannot

be so in form. 'Commands', however determinate their source, have an indeterminacy of form that threatens regulation and coordination. Command is acceptable if law is to be like the Decalogue with a determinate superior added, but not if its task is to facilitate the interaction of numerous and complexly related spheres of activity and agents within them. It follows that the public power must itself take a rule-governed and relatively predictable form; the question is not merely identifying the 'sovereign' by rules of recognition but of ensuring that the 'sovereign's legislation is of some social utility. That is, because the regulating action of the public power is itself codified, then its enactments are not merely knowable as such, as 'laws', but are sufficiently non-capricious that they do indeed serve to regulate the affairs of a complex society.

The Roman Empire is the first fully recognizable legal order. Its later rulers claimed a 'sovereignty' sufficient to please the most hardened Austinian. Its legislation was dominated by the principle that 'the ruler's will has the force of law'. Through the fiction of the *Lex Regia* the Emperor claimed an absolutism sufficient for the most desperate Hobbist. But what is regulated by such laws is a complex multi-national assemblage of citizens, cities, corporations and associations. The Emperor's will is the source of law, but if the Emperor's word is law it is only so in a meaningful sense, possessing social utility, if that word takes the form of law and not whims or merely particular commands. The elaboration and codification of Roman Law represent a continued effort to meet this standard, despite considerable instability and periods of arbitrary rule.

3   Such an interacting set of realms of differentiated agencies of decision needs to be regulated, but it can never be reduced to the equivalent of a group of persons bound by exhaustive repertoires of prescribed conduct. The interaction of distinct realms and the differentiation of independent agents necessarily give rise to conflicting interests between and within realms. A society with a legal order necessarily exhibits the conflict of interests; such systematic conflict and its regulation are simply different aspects of the same phenomenon. Therefore, even in a society with a supreme and all-powerful ruler like the Roman Emperor there will be conflict and its intellectual reflection. A legal order has always implied alternatives within itself – different conceptions of the political form and function of that order. Law is about public issues in a legal order, not merely a set of closed rules for governing individual conduct. In this sense, since the very beginning of jurisprudence there have been options and arguments as to the form and content of law. Legal reasoning has existed to debate the public issues that arise from the conflicting interests. Since at least the days of Bartolus of Sassaferrato Western jurisprudence has been characterized

by open critical debate. The critical legal studies movement is thus the latest in a long line of disputes and conflicts within the reasoning which is a necessary part of a legal order. Even when jurists were faced with debating the respective claims to absolute and illimitable authority on the part of the Empire and the Papacy, there were arguments between these powers and on behalf of lesser powers, such as the free Italian cities.

We can see therefore that the single public power may not be liberal pluralist in the modern sense but that it exists because of a complex plurality of activities, associations and agents. A legal order is necessarily bound up with a certain degree of social pluralism. Absolutist jurisprudence from Bodin and Hobbes to Austin succeeded in clearly formulating the claims of that single public power in the form of the modern state. In conceiving of 'sovereignty' it accomplished this task exceedingly well but at the expense of neglecting to conceptualize the social pluralism which is the very *raison d'être* of a legal order. It would be a pity if we were to make exactly the opposite error, that in our hostility to political power unjustly, excessively and oppressively used we reject the concept of legal order and in so doing are driven to deny the social pluralism on which it is based. Modern societies are unlikely to become less institutionally complex, less socially differentiated and more morally homogeneous than the Roman Empire. If that is so then such societies cannot dispense with a legal order; only a simple communalistic society without complex social division of labour and with a single and tyranically prescriptive moral code can do that. If anyone wants such a society in the name of socialism, anarchism, feminism or ecologism then they must set an absolute zero value on human freedom. Freedom only exists because of the messy conflict of independent agencies and their distinct interests. It is sustainable and tolerable, as *freedom*, only when contained by legal regulation.

We have a choice between building on the conceptual achievements of liberalism and pluralism or talking nonsense – in other words no choice at all. Liberal pluralism tries to express the forms of political/ legal organization consistent with the plurality of agencies and associations that makes regulation necessary. It challenges absolutist jurisprudence. The public power must not only regulate but answer to society, and it also demands from the agents and associations some minimum level of commitment to the norms necessary to a pluralist society and polity. Liberal pluralism is a critical challenge to a certain conception of the state and to a certain conception of social agents: to absolutism (whether legitimated by democracy or not), and also to economic liberalism which puts the freedom to buy and sell above a morally sustainable and politically democratic social order. Liberal political jurisprudence is far from an uncritical justification of the *status quo*; it is a body of thought which can both challenge and build on the political and legal world we inhabit and does not need to deny it in the service of some supposed 'alternative'.

Liberal pluralism advances a number of propositions which it is difficult to challenge and they point to the gains and advantages of a liberal democratic political-legal order which cannot be supplanted, only destroyed or replaced by second-best substitutes. We will summarize these in a set of claims.

A legal order depends on the existence of the state: therefore to supplant formal law is also to abolish the state as a separate public power. This is, in effect, to raise the question of the withering away of the state. We have seen that a complex society with social differentiation and divison of labour requires a separate public power as a condition of the interaction of the components of its 'civil society'. If we seek to abolish formal law, as some radical critics do, then we have a choice between anything approaching civilization and a simple stateless society, which can dispense with a legal order. The issue for any serious radical is the *form* of state and law, and not the existence of the state. A legal order is not coextensive with and definitive of the state. A stateless society in the modern world is an illusion. We cannot 'abolish' the state. But we should be careful to note that although a form of state is necessary to a legal order, states and legal regulations are not the same thing. States have other conditions of existence than the need to give sanction to the judgements of law. States arise from and to further political struggle. No theory of the legal order, no liberal vision of political organization can survive as a serious challenge to political realism if it ignores the challenge of friend–enemy relations and unless it makes an effort to explain how such political struggle can be minimized and contained. This cannot be done by liberal-constitutionalist dogmas alone, but by specific *political* provision. This is the challenge of Carl Schmitt's authoritarian conservative jurisprudence. *The Concept of the Political* needs to be mastered by liberal-pluralist jurisprudence, not ignored as illiberal and reactionary.

A pluralistic 'civil society' requires for its regulation at minimum a *Rechtsstaat* and some elaborated rule of recognition, that not merely identifies the source of law but also requires that legislation and legal norms take the form of being a 'law'. Such an ordered society is perfectly compatible with authoritarian rather than democratic political rule. A 'pluralistic' civil society is matched by a pluralistic political system only when the following conditions are met:

1   A number of distinct and legitimate political forces compete to influence the public power and continue to enjoy such a measure of influence that they remain in the competition. Distinctive political parties competing in democratic elections are merely one crucial subset

of such relatively open political competition.

2 The pluralism of political-organizational competition is based on and derives its support from a broader associational pluralism. Social activities are organized by bodies formed by freely associated citizens and whilst these are regulated by the public power they act as independent agents and are not directed in their actions by it.

3 No large body of adult citizens exclusively defined by certain attributes is denied by the public power the capacity to engage in political competition and the freedom to form associations.

4 No body of citizens is so subordinated to any other citizen or association as a condition of earning their livelihood that they lack the capacity to enter political competition or form associations as agents in their own right. It follows that a pluralistic polity is one where laws need to meet a double substantive test: they must command assent from diverse active and influential agents and associations, and they must not only have utility in furthering the effective interaction of agents and associations but must not systematically subordinate without good cause any group of agents and associations in doing so. It should be evident to anybody who reads this that much legislation simply fails this double test in the West today. To meet this test laws and legal norms must be relatively elaborated rules and provisions, assessed and debated before being put into effect, and overseen in their application by competent specialists. Only on the basis of a degree of certainty of content and consistency of application can they be known to be equitable enough in their actions to command consent.

This requirement explains why the legal order of a pluralistic society cannot tolerate a large amount of informal justice and ad hoc adjudication and arbitration. The framework of interaction of groups, associations and agents must be sufficiently predictable that agents can rely on the public power and on others. Trust of others and assent to authority require a measure of certainty. Kadi justice is intolerable in defining central aspects of the legal order of liberal-pluralist society. Some pluralists and critics of the centralized and hierarchical state in attacking 'sovereignty' challenge the idea of a legal order with formal rules and functionally competent specialists as well. G. D. H. Cole in his Guild Socialist phase is a good example of a social theorist who sought to retain the benefits of modern industry, division of labour and social pluralism without a separate public power.[7] His answer to problems of regulation and the determination of the limits of competence was a 'court of functional equity', that would sort out by ad hoc decisions all the conflicts that would inevitably arise between the different functionally specific associations. Recently John Burnheim has virtually re-invented Cole's functional democracy and with it ad hoc arbitration by courts manned by non-specialists.[8] Far from supplanting the sovereign state and formal law these 'alternatives' need the supplement of aspects of the thing rejected, except that law and legal regulation reappear in forms less adequate and appropriate. Figgis was never so naive; nor was Maitland. They envisaged sovereignty in a pluralist state, not the virtual abolition of a separate public power.

Law is not merely a constraint externally imposed on associations and agents; it provides an intelligible guide to action for those agents. Law provides not merely the conditions of compliance, but the intellectual means to anticipate and predict, to extend conduct to analogous situations. Modern social pluralism has been accompanied by, and in a considerable measure produced by, advanced individuation. Initially such individuation developed in Christian congregations, particularly in the seventeenth century, on the basis of a personal relation to God, and the control of conduct through introspection and 'conscience'. From God's Law it has been extended to civil laws and social conduct in general. H. L. A. Hart is correct to stress the real gains that emerge when the subjects of the law adopt an 'internal point of view' and become citizens and social agents who internalize the laws as valid rules for their own conduct. In this circumstance law becomes an automatic technology of the agent's calculation. It permits, for example, complex and large-scale associations both to function internally and to interact with others with a minimum of friction and a minimum of constraint on the part of the public power. Hart's concept is a valuable tool of criticism in that so much of our legislation and regulation spurns the internal point of view; it regards the subjects of law with suspicion and contempt. The concept also serves as a devastating critique of any form of legally sustained social discrimination. The 'internal point of view' is often less a description of many individuals' relations to the law than something to be constructed in a liberal-pluralist citizenry by economic, social and legal reform. It implies a well-educated, economically secure and politically influential populace who can identify with political authority and can accept and use the law as a technology for action. This is self-evidently not the case for many people in Britain or the USA today.

In this highly abstract and ideal–typical analysis of pluralist legal order, the state as a separate public power has a limited set of functions. Its task is to regulate the interaction of agents and associations. No reference has been made to the state as an omnicompetent administrative machine organizing and providing for diverse social needs and activities. The liberal-pluralist legal order does not have an easy place for what Carl Schmitt called the 'total state'. The 'pluralist' theory of the state and associations advanced by such thinkers as Figgis and Maitland did not do this because of some oversight but because they placed a primary value on the freedom of agents and associations. The 'total state' has emerged from the dual pressures of mass industrial warfare and the consequent mobilization of all social and economic resources for 'total war', and from democratic demands for social welfare and greater equality in access to health, education, housing, etc.

Ultimately, such a 'total state' is incompatible with a liberal-pluralist order. It is virtually incapable of political supervision and it confronts citizens and free associations of citizens as a power they can barely challenge, and uses its continued adoption of a formally *Rechtsstaatlich* character as one more device to subordinate. This fact implies taking the pluralist theory of associations and of the role of the public power in a society of associations seriously. For the pluralists, 'civil society' is a society of associations, not of atomized individuals. Associations freely formed of citizens should perform all major tasks of social life – production, distribution, education, etc. That implies limits to the purely private accumulation and ownership of economically productive wealth – firms should be cooperative or associative. Such a system implies genuine options for members of society and a definite but containable public power. That power permits the interaction of associations and does not attempt to supplant them. As a theory it is the only realistic answer to the 'total state'; 'big government' cannot be contained by the measures proposed by the liberal constitutionalist theory of representative government. If we are to enjoy the benefits of modern industry, division of labour and freedom of association, we cannot 'smash' the state. If we expect it to perform every social function and administer every activity we cannot expect genuine democratic control, only a plebiscitarian formal legitimation of administration. The only answer is to limit the state to tasks that it can perform, and that 'civil society' can accept and give assent to without being crushed.

To create the state of the pluralist theory of associations three conditions need to be satisfied.

1   The reduction of international tensions to a level where external defence ceases to be a primary call on the organizational skills and economic resources of society, where political authority need not be ever more centralized in the ruthless pursuit of military success.

2   Either major sources of inter-group and inter-associational conflict are eliminated, or a strong consensus is built to sustain those norms of political life which effectively constrain those groups which reject and seek to overthrow the pluralist framework. Carl Schmitt pointed to this dilemma, a dilemma in the liberal concept of basic freedoms of political action; that is, there needs must be a constitutional defence of, and therefore suspension of, those freedoms against agents and groups who use them in order to establish a non-pluralist regime. The public power must therefore be able to contain and deny an 'equal chance' to those forces that seek to overthrow the existing order. This dilemma is most

acute in a 'total state' within a parliamentary-democratic framework. The stakes of winning are immense – a group can use political freedoms in order to deny others an equal chance to compete for power and also, by using virtually unlimited state power once it has won an election, suppress political competition as such. In a pluralist state, as advocated by Figgis, the stakes of victory are much less; the state has essentially a regulatory function and it faces a highly organized civil society of active and powerful associations.

3   Strict limits are placed on the forms of ownership permitted for economically productive wealth and on the extent to which any coopera- tive or association may control its sphere of economic activity.

These conditions are difficult to satisfy but they are not impossible in the way Marxism's communist utopia is. Furthermore, failure to satisfy them does not invalidate other aspects of pluralist theory or reduce its critical power.

The political pluralism of Figgis clearly implies a minimum social morality necessary to support the legal regulation of group interaction; groups must accept the validity of other associations freely formed of citizens doing things as they wish. This minimum is actually rather a lot. It implies acceptance of ethical pluralism and the acceptance of parallel associations and groups doing things their own way. It therefore excludes 'totalizing' ethical projects that seek to subordinate the con- duct of others to their rule. Outside of an irreducible minimum of criminal laws, agents' and associations' conducts would have to be tolerated and at best preached against. Some religious groups and some forms of 'lifestyle politics' would find this ethical pluralism hard to accept and might well fall under a version of the constitutional defence of the 'equal chance' we outlined above. No society can exist without some measure of force and the suppression of some of the options for conduct some of its members may envisage. The defence of ethical pluralism against moral totalitarianism seems to us no great loss. Ethical pluralism is another of the unsupplantable gains of the liberal pluralist tradition in jurisprudence.

The pluralist theory implies radical changes in political and social institutions but it is not utopian in the way that the ultimate post- political goals of Marxism are. In a society with widespread inequality in political, economic and educational resources pluralism would actually be pernicious, for it would cement and enhance the autonomy of the well endowed. In a society falling far short of a substantial measure of equality on the part of its citizens, public provision to meet needs and counteract unequal distribution will remain essential. The great advan- tage of pluralist theory, however, is that it does not depend on all-or-nothing revolution in social organization. The pluralization of political authority, the creation of a multi-centred state with distinct functionally specific dimensions of authority, and the pluralization of social relations, the transfer of functions to cooperative and association-al institutions, could proceed in a relatively piecemeal manner.

Pluralism is not trapped in a contradiction of political action which has bedevilled Marxist states and which has been ably deliniated by Chen Erjin.[9] Erjin demonstrates that the Marxist theory of class struggle and the dictatorship of the proleteriat requires the ruthless concentra-tion of state power to crush 'class enemies'. That concentration, however, inhibits the Marxist goal of a freer society based on the self-action of the people which would be necessary for the construction of non-authoritarian socialism. The socialist state, if it ruthlessly pursues the 'dictatorship of the proleteriat', pulverizes and disables civil society and tends to convert all those who challenge it in the name of freedom into enemies. Pluralism, on the contrary, moves in an opposite direction and enables diverse political and social forces. It permits diverse forms of economic and social organization, diverse aims and ideals. Plural-ism's foes are threefold: centralized state power ruthlessly pursuing international conflicts and the internal 'pacification' necessary to further them; unequal concentrations of the productive wealth of society directed in an authoritarian manner; and religious/ethical movements which seek to impose one prescriptive moral code of conduct on all. As such it can appeal widely and to all who, whatever their other disagreements, put the freedom of citizens and freely formed associa-tions first in their order of social values. The project of a pluralist politics and the creation of a pluralist legal order in an advanced liberal society provide a valid basis for a jurisprudence that can challenge authoritarian socialism and (barely) liberal capitalism. It draws on central aspects of established Western jurisprudence for its tools of criticism and its proposals for change.

5

Associational socialism in a pluralist state

Why continue to write about the legal order of a socialist society? Surely the only future socialism has is the futile one of politically impotent intellectuals speculating on 'the future of socialism'? Like any social and political idea, socialism requires a social and political force capable of putting it into effect. But the 'proletariat' has always been a phantasm created by the intelligentsia, and the 'working class' – a slightly more credible phenomenon created by industrialization and by the Labour Movement – has dissolved with socio-economic differentiation into mutually indifferent fragments.[1]

A centrally planned socialism effects a convenient union of the intelligentsia and the working class. It is a system in which the intellectuals are essential in organizing a society for the benefit of the producers. But how to sell such an idea in the advanced Western industrial countries today? The intelligentsia has been marginalized and deprived of functions by mass culture and mass administration. More numerous than ever, it is powerless as never before. The intelligentsia talks to itself in its specialized ghettos. What happens to the 'producers' in a society where production is mechanized and socialized on the basis of private property, in which the productivity of modern industry has revolutionized labour? Producers are everywhere, in the complex processes of planning, design, administration and marketing, and also nowhere; 'labour' counts for less and less in the productive process and is replaced by a series of specialized and hierarchical roles. A large proportion of the population is not economically active, and of the economically active only a small proportion are manual workers in manufacturing industry. A society organized for the benefit of produ-cers is less and less attractive. Industrial workers are no longer part of the starveling masses but relatively well-paid specialists. In a representative democracy a party addressing itself to manual workers and claiming to represent a strong form of producer-oriented socialism will never become more than a marginalizable minority.[2]

Should we, then, conclude that socialism is dead? Is it an idea created by the First Industrial Revolution that has become absurd in the Third? The intellectual right would have us believe so and have made as much play with the death of socialism in the 1980s as liberal theologians did with the death of God in the 1960s. The socialisms attacked here are those of a collectivist economy, in which central planning decisions are substituted for the price mechanism, and a collectivist society of bureaucratic regulation and administered welfare. The radical right strikes simultaneously against Soviet socialism and against Keynes/Beveridge inspired social democracy. Is socialism slain by this double blow? Well not exactly, because the targets represent no more than a fraction of the socialisms created in the last two centuries. And yet a problem remains, because Soviet socialism and Western social democracy have been the two politically dominant and most politically successful forms of socialism.

The Soviet model of central planning is almost universally unpopular in the West. Western social democratic and socialist parties are, by and large, confined to definite electoral niches, seldom commanding a majority of the vote. Socialist parties may from governments, but these governments cannot attempt to introduce socialism. They lack the overwhelming majority of electoral support necessary to make that project legitimate. The socialisms untouched by the rightist criticism are the ones beaten into marginality by their more successful opponents in the late nineteenth century and early twentieth century – associationalist, cooperative and syndicalist socialisms.[3] Perhaps the right can safely ignore them because they are irrelevant? Well not exactly, because the collectivist socialisms were dominant and most successful precisely at the apogee of the labour movement and of 'working class' mass parties. In the period of the decline of collectivism aspects of the 'other' socialisms became relevant as never before, because they raise questions of the democratic organization of society which are now vital.

The right, in preaching the death of socialism, offers individual choice in a free market as an alternative to regulation, bureaucracy and administrative fiat. However, the result of the apparent dominance of the market is, on the contrary, the private domination of hierarchically directed unaccountable agencies with great economic and political power – financial and industrial corporations. Deregulated markets, far from being 'free', are politically beneficial to these corporations, which enjoy the unequal advantages of the price-making and privileged information. Whilst these corporations may compete one with another on relatively equal terms, all other economic actors simply have to accept the results of their competitive action. In partnership with the corporations in the rightist's market society is a state not the less powerful for having ceded certain regulatory functions and economic activities. On the contrary, state power is concentrated as never before and enjoys a repressive capacity hitherto undreamed of. The role of democracy in such a state is that of a plebiscite which legitimates the actions of the administration. The right offers, in practice, the dual role of the unaccountable private government of the corporations and the – at best – formally democratic government of the state. As a mechanism of this dual rule there is 'the market'; markets dictate whatever cannot be legitimated politically as an economic *fait accompli*. 'The market' is far from being a single entity, nor is it a neutral social mechanism, equally open to all participants. The key *markets* – in national currencies, government bonds, equities and basic commodities – are both publicly organized and dominated by small numbers of privileged actors.

In terms of the values of liberalism, individual freedom and self-action to which the right appeal, the dominance of the 'free' market means, in practice, the domination of unaccountable managements, using market mechanisms to pursue their control of economic activity. Liberal democratic values are negated by the private governments of corporations that impose hierarchy, loyalty and obedience on those who work for them, and which impose market outcomes on all agents who lack their economic power. If socialism has any relevance today, it is by raising the two linked questions of the democratic governance of private corporations and the democratization of state administration. Only by acting in conformity with the dominant values which stress individual choice and self-action can socialists hope to offer a doctrine that has takers outside of committed but ineffectual intellectuals and the now shrunken hard core of the Labour Movement.

Centrally planned socialist economies – that is, economies in which the whole economy is supposed to be planned by state decision-making agencies and in which administered prices corresponding to plan objectives are substituted for 'free'-market mechanisms – have no political appeal as alternatives to corporate capitalism. Leaving aside the technical questions of whether such an economy is actually possible in the strict sense, the very rough approximations to it in the USSR and Eastern Europe have proven themselves extremely inefficient and have failed to compete with the West in technological development, productivity and consumer choice. Corporate capitalist economies do better, even though they are as far from the abstract model of a perfectly free market as the lumbering mass of ministries and planning agencies in the Soviet Union is from the even less realizable model of an efficient planned economy. The reason is that the organization of the economy into private corporations, however undemocratic their internal management, decentralizes the process of decision-making and simplifies the requirements of information-gathering. An efficient centralized and planned economy would imply the centralization and inter-meshing of information and decisions. It would inevitably concentrate economic and political power. Distinct interests, alternatives and policy options would have to be eliminated or restricted even if political authority were formally democratic and if there were free public discussion and majority voting on what to choose. To Western publics, committed to liberalism, individualism and pluralism, central planning is a political abomination, even if it were technically much more efficient and a great deal less authoritarian than it is in the USSR. Socialism has nothing to gain from contrasting the efficiency of planning with waste and anarchy of the market.

Associational socialism always pre-supposed the plurality and autonomy of enterprises and other collective bodies as decision-making agencies. It assumed a system of cooperatively and associatively owned agencies that were to be managed by procedures which depended on democratic consent. Where possible cooperation and association were to link these agencies one to another, rather than exchange relationships and market competition. Traditional associational socialism was producer-oriented and a doctrine of the self-management of the working class. It is readily adaptable, however, to much more complex societies, which are no longer dominated by relatively low technology factories and which have a complex and differentiated occupational structure in place of a 'working class'. Associational socialism is adaptable to hospitals, universities, and shopping centres, as much as it is to factories. It is compatible with complex forms of social ownership, in which workers, providers of capital and other interests are represented on a democratic board of management. By its very principle it permits diversity in forms of organization and management of enterprises.

Associational socialism addresses the problems of hierarchy and administrative centralization in enterprises and collective bodies. It argues for the democratization of corporations. It permits and encourages the associationalization of social life: education, health, welfare, community services can be provided by cooperatively or socially owned and democratically managed bodies. It permits such bodies to set their own objectives. It is thus compatible with a pluralistic society in which there are distinct sets of values and organized interests. It can tolerate and, indeed, should welcome the Catholic Church and the gay community, for example, providing health and welfare services for their members. Obviously, it will not seek to nationalize the corner shop, or regiment the independent artisan, although it provides the framework in which shopkeepers and artisans can create their own associations of mutual assistance. A socialism in which there is room only for committed socialists of the traditional type will never get off first base. Associational socialism builds on – rather than negating – the plurality and diversity of Western civil society; it enhances the powers of voluntary associations and communities. Unlike the economic totalitarianism of central planning, it is not condemned to marginalize associations and deny them decision-making autonomy. Unlike the domination of market-oriented corporate capitalism it does not push associations to the 'social' margins, away from economic market-oriented activity.

Associational socialism is thus closer to the traditions of Western pluralism and liberalism than are the doctrines of either the central planners of the free-marketeers. It recognizes in the private and unaccountable power of corporations a threat to democracy and individual liberty, not only in the sphere of economic relations but in the capacity of corporate management to set the social and political agenda. Societies in which the power of economic decision-making is so concentrated cannot be fully democratic.

A society in which the basic units are democratically managed associations nevertheless requires mechanisms of interaction between them, and the regulation of that interaction. The basic units cannot be left to associate spontaneously and manage themselves, except on the assumptions of a basic homogeneity of aim and identity of interests. It was just these assumptions that made Syndicalism and Guild Socialism so unrealistic, being based on a mentality of producerism and workerism, which supposed a unitary 'working class'. On the assumptions of a plurality of aims and divergence of interests, then inter-associational interaction cannot simply be a matter of mutual consent.

Likewise it is equally naive to suppose that once the economic actors have been appropriately defined and have been socialized, it is possible to rely on the free competitive market. This is the chief error of most market socialists, who believe the central proposition of neo-classical economics that the closer a market approaches perfection, the more efficient an allocative mechanism it is. A perfectly competitive market, whatever its value as an abstract device of economic theory, is a social impossibility. Therefore, markets as media of interaction of enterprises require careful regulation if the associational basis of the social order is to be maintained. Unregulated competition and an open market in associations' or cooperatives' shares would lead back to corporate capitalism in short order. The growth of enterprises and the operation of capital markets need to be monitored and controlled. However, markets assigned to particular enterprises and the tight direction of capital funds by some central agency would rapidly lead to stagnation and petty local monopolies – a world like the medieval guilds.

An associational society needs, therefore, regulation and supra-enterprise services and agencies in order to function. Like all socialisms – doctrines concerned to govern the economy in the interests of a certain conception of the social order – associational socialism extends the scope and range of state activity. Such a socialism cannot be 'planned', however, to guarantee desirable aggregate outcomes from the activity of associations or to preserve and protect every association. Competition may be regulated but it will not be eliminated. Associations, agencies and their members will not be equally successful or enjoy equal rewards. They will not even enjoy equal access to resources. This is inevitable in any system where agencies are relatively free to make decisions. A world of equality of outcomes and an absolutely equal chance to compete is unattainable, if one values autonomy and self-management. But if one does value autonomy and self-management, then it is also true that failure cannot be permitted to become absolute and self-perpetuating as far as individuals are concerned. Associations and enterprises may fail; individuals, however, must find a net of income support and training sufficient to re-start them and prevent themselves and their children becoming a pauper class. Where possible this support and training should be provided by associations and not by conventional state agencies.

An associationalist society cannot be a stateless commonwealth or a pure democracy of associations. As a plurality of realms of agencies of decision, it requires a legal order and a legal order requires a public power in some form.[4] Associational socialism is committed to the project of developing a certain form of social order. It therefore requires a public power with the collective agencies and the funds to supervise associations and provide services to enable them to fulfil their roles. An associationalist social order is incompatible with a highly centralized, bureaucratically organized and omnicompetent 'total state'. Such a state, even if it has representative-democratic procedures for the selection of governing personnel, represents a concentration of decision-making and administrative power at variance with the very principle of associationalism. If such a state is hierarchically organized and, in theory, directed from a single authoritative centre, it may be democratically legitimated but it is not democratically managed. If it is a party state it gives the leaders a narrow majority (say 51 per cent) the capacity to determine how others shall live by means of its powers of legislation and capacities of administration.

Associationalist socialism implies a pluralism of values, agencies and enterprises that requires for its regulation a legal order and public power, but that pluralism can be undermined by an authoritarian state power. An associationalist society demands an elaborate programme of regulation, supervision and support from the public power but it must be a power adapted to the new tasks. A society of democratic associations requires a state which not only shares the attributes of civil society, that is, pluralism and democratic self-management, but to a degree merges with it. In such a complex and differentiated society communication between administrative organs of state and the social bodies must be close if regulative acts and decisions are to reflect the needs of associations. At the same time, the public power must have that degree of separation from and superiority over the associations which is necessary to sustain an independent legal order that oversees their actions and is not unduly subject to the associations' influence and pressure. The implication is a pluralistic state in the sense used by John Neville Figgis.[5] Such a state has a complex and multiform structure, with distinct, functionally separate forms and levels of authority, in which there is no fiction of a single 'sovereign'.

Pluralism is difficult to define as a political and legal doctrine.[6] Sometimes it has amounted to no more than a challenge to some of the more extreme versions of the doctrine of state sovereignty, which are only modernizations of the claims of royal absolutism. Sometimes it has been carried to virtual incoherence by making the assumption that the state is merely one association among others, and that its claims to obedience are no more overriding than those of other associations. This is the great defect of the earlier work of Harold Laski. In the one case a mild form of federalism with a written constitution limiting the powers of legislature and executive would appear to be enough to constitute a pluralist state. In the other case the state becomes indistinguishable, except for certain specialist functions, from any other association. It is like a football club, but one that prints money and has an army! Critics like K. C. Hsiao in *Political Pluralism* (1927) found it easy to show that in this latter extreme form, pluralism negated the very idea of a legal order; pluralism in this sense is ultimately fictitious because every legal order must claim primacy and obligatoriness in its own domain.

This is true, but not every state has to claim a 'sovereignty' that implies an unchallengeable plenitude of power. Nor does it have to claim that it is the sole legitimate and continuing association and that all other associations exist by its legal fiat and tolerance alone. J. N. Figgis, in *Churches in the Modern State*, showed the disastrous consequences of these doctrines for associational life in his analysis of the Free Church of Scotland case.[7] Figgis made clear that associations must be regulated by laws, that law is central to ordered associational life, and that the public power, insofar as it sustains the legal order, is not just one association among others, but the association of associations. But the law should recognize associations as continuing collective agencies with a right to develop and determine their own purposes, and not treat them as mere legal fictions and as deriving their existence solely from their articles of incorporation. A pluralist state would therefore be one whose constitution and legislation recognized not only individual citizens but also associations as part of its own order. A pluralist state defines its *raison d'être* as the assistance and supervision of associations. Its legal task is to ensure equity between associations and to police the conduct of associations. It treats both individuals and associations as real persons, recognizes that individuals can only pursue individualization and fulfil themselves through association with others, and accepts that it must protect the rights of both individuals and associations and seek to control misconduct.

A state which builds associations into its own order through representative and consultative mechanisms, which disperses its administrative apparatus through distinct, functionally specific domains of authority, which is decentralized, and which permits its servants a measure of democratic self-management, is a pluralist state. Its legislature will reflect in its composition that state's own internal complexity and that of society, but within the limits of the pluralist constitution it will have full powers to make legal provision. Its judiciary, likewise, will be independent and able to judge associations' claims and conducts according to law. Hsiao's criticisms, therefore, are beside the point; a pluralist state will claim legislative sovereignty *within its own constitutional limits and objectives*, that is where the difference lies, for it is these limits and objectives which redefine the content of sovereignty.

A pluralist state is the antidote to the most undesirable aspects of modern state power. The modern state claims a monopoly of the means of violence in a definite territory which is its exclusive possession. It claims legislative primacy, that is, to be the sole source and agency of binding rules within its territory, and claims to hold the right to determine the legitimacy of all activities in that territory. Furthermore, it presents itself as a single 'sovereign' public power and it has a distinct bureaucratic administrative machine separated from the other activities of society. It also generally claims to rule by popular consent and to submit its activities to the rule of law. Even allowing for this latter claim, the state is a compulsory organization that treats its own territory and its population as subject to its own control and direction. The more liberal and democratic the state, the more plausible will be the claim that control and direction are both formally lawful and supported by popular consent. A pluralist state must inevitably make some of these claims, if, in some cases, with a modified content and a lessened force.

To the extent that a state is confronted with powerful antagonistic interests in civil society, it must stress its separateness, its monopoly of force and its primary role in determining the legitimacy of conduct. To the extent that a state is confronted with powerful external forces, it must stress the exclusiveness of its possession of a distinct territory and it must stress its right to call on the lives and resources of all persons within its territory in case of war. To the extent that it is confronted with powerful hierarchically directed organizations, such as business corporations, it must stress the doctrine that they are creatures of law and that their existence is subject ultimately to its will.

Pluralism precisely sets out to minimize the extent of each of these exigencies. Pluralism and associational socialism operate to reduce the antagonism of interests in civil society through allowing organizations distinct domains of activity and self-government and by reducing hierarchy and direction by managerial imperatives. Private hierarchies encourage antagonistic interests by creating subordinates and superordinates and they force the state to adopt similar administrative forms in order to respond to them with equal authoritativeness. Military organization is the most typical form of authoritarian hierarchy, the very model of gradations of ranks issuing orders to those below. A pluralistic state of necessity implies a condition of lessened international tension and a minimum call on the resources of society to provide for and to submit to hierarchical military force.

Most socialists have envisaged a socialist society as one without a plurality of distinct interests and as so homogeneous that there is but one scale of values and objectives. This is true not only of Marxist believers in central planning but also of most associational socialists. In the latter case a mixture of workerism and a belief in the direct democracy of the association led them to attach little value to distinct state institutions and formal legal codes. Given such homogeneity, such socialists supposed that democracy above the associational level presents few problems; it can be a relatively ad hoc matter, settled by the meeting of representatives of associations. Indeed, it was the failure to see that an associational society allows great diversity of organizational forms, great complexity in the interaction of associations, and the coexistence of very different values and objectives that led these associational socialists naively to believe that a legal order and a distinct public power could be virtually dispensed with. Associations may differ on most things and to the extent that a pluralist state grants them genuine autonomy, they may organize their affairs in very different ways. In this case, not only is the legal institutionalization and regulation of associations necessary, but it is a precondition of the stable interaction of associations. Associationalism requires the state as a separate public power precisely because of the social pluralism it allows to develop to the full.

Antagonism between associations is as possible as that between class-representative political parties. How then can it be prevented from destroying the social order? As the American pluralists discovered, distinct and competing interests can serve as one of the foundations of democracy, if they are made an explicit part of the political process and if their members subscribe to the values of democratic political competition. Plural interests counter-balance one another.[8] Doubtless, in an associational system, if, for example, the gay community and the Catholic Church both have a legitimate place, they will run their own organizations very differently, will have very different educational or welfare objectives, and very different rules of personal conduct. A pluralist system that cannot accommodate the two, that cannot allow both to undertake major tasks of social organization, as the primary providers of services to their members, is clearly doomed.

Associations may have a pretty low opinion of one another, but a pluralist state will only work if there are effective institutions that promote their mutual tolerance, if not approval. There are three main ways this can be done. The first is to impose minimum standards of provision of services and conduct on all associations, to be agreed in a legislature where associations are represented. The supervision and enforcement of such agreement requires independent legal institutions. A religious group can condemn sodomy – if its members accept this rule of conduct so be it – but the group cannot impose it upon others or punish their own members guilty of such conduct beyond a certain limit. The second method is to ensure that a range of associations is adequately funded to ensure certain services; the state would thus not only regulate but provide finance for associational projects. The wider the range of associations, the greater the chance of diluting the conflict of the ones that are most antagonistic by means of relatively 'neutral' agencies and by providing relatively 'neutral' let-outs for individuals. In the case of education, for example, there might be Catholic schools and gay universities, but also associations simply devoted to providing education with no explicit political and social programme, such as parent/teacher school cooperatives. Thirdly, a pluralistic polity need not be built on associations alone. A legislature, for example, could be multi-cameral, with a corporatist element – a chamber representing associations, a representative democratic element – a chamber representing individuals elected by territorial constituencies, and a deliberative specialist element – a chamber representing chosen notables with special experience or knowledge.

A *purely* associational society could easily degenerate into a series of petty tyrannies, each at war with one another. Individuals' associational memberships may well be plural and functionally specific; thus someone may belong to the Catholic Church for purposes of worship but not for most social activities. A state which did not protect individuals by imposing on associations degrees of membership and by making sure that relatively neutral alternatives were available may be pluralistic in form but would permit associations to practise a form of totalitarianism.

Traditionally, associationalist socialism stressed direct democracy and self-management, the immediate involvement of producers in their primary associations. Certainly, one should stress the value of self-management, but also note its organizational limitations and costs. Most citizens will seek 'limited liability' in the matter of political involvement. Associationalism need not depend wholly on direct democracy and self-management as a doctrine. If it did, it would be fatally flawed and unable to deal with problems of complex and large-scale organization. Associations may combine direct and representative democracy, self- and specialist management. A management board of an enterprise would be representative-democratic, with various constituencies of interest represented (the various grades of workers/cooperators, the suppliers of external capital, the local community, etc.), other aspects of work organization a matter of combining specialist direction and direct democracy (an autonomous work-group would be given specifications and deadlines by specialist production managers, for example). The great bugbears of any attempt to democratize institutions – brain-surgery by committee, having to live like a party activist for fifty years, and so on – can be avoided. Most associations, most of the time, would be run by specialists and activists. This presents few problems if there is the possibility of mass democratic input and if there are other parallel associations to which members may go if dissatisfied.

An associationalist society would be complex; it would permit private property; it would be far from a levelling equality; it would involve conflict – but it would radically reduce the scope for hierarchy and for authoritarian administration, whether state or private in character. It would be a system in which law and legal regulation were central to social organization. It would involve a state with an elaborate formal constitution. It would be quite unlike a socialist utopia. Indeed, its citizens would probably not use the word 'socialism' to describe it and they would certainly not be required to subscribe to any official ideology. If they were expected to believe in anything, it would be the virtues of democratic organization, the superiority of free associations as the basis for providing goods and services and the values of individual freedom and tolerance of others. In other words, it would involve no violent break with the traditions of Western democracy and liberalism, constitutional government and the rule of law. The only things it would have eliminated are large autocratically directed private accumulations of wealth, and state and private hierarchies in which it is the subordinate's job only to obey.

Associational socialism and the theory of the pluralist state offer the best chance of continuing the nineteenth-century project of socialism into the twenty-first century. That project had many strands and variants. One thing they all stressed was the disastrous consequences of the dominance of politics and society by the economic doctrines of *laissez faire*. The pursuit of 'private' economic interest in an 'open' market will neither guarantee adequate outcomes for social justice, nor will it preserve a desirable social order. On the contrary, it tends to subordinate the political objectives of liberalism, of democracy and of egalitarianism to the economic needs of powerful and undemocratically managed collective agencies – business corporations. Socialism has suffered precisely because it attempted to answer the economic failings of capitalistic *laissez faire* with collectivism and workerism. Because these, too, acted not merely to subordinate but to destroy the liberal-democratic order wherever they were put most fully into effect, socialism has receded in those countries where the social democratic synthesis of democracy and corporate capitalism managed to keep the ravages of unregulated capitalism to a tolerable level. That synthesis is now threatened. Social democracy finds itself threatened precisely because it is no longer necessary as a political competitor to authoritarian socialism and because modern societies no longer periodically require the mobilization of all social resources to effectively meet the demands of industrialized mass warfare. The labour of many has now become marginal and there is less to fear from the dissatisfaction of an economically disadvantaged underclass.

The privatizers and deregulators are, however, trading on the capital of the social democratic synthesis and they are squandering it recklessly in the interests of the corporate wealthy. They can count for the time being on a considerable degree of popular support, but only up to and not beyond the dismantling of the liberal-collectivist apparatuses of health, education and welfare. They can count on support for inequality, but only up to and not beyond the point where tax cuts, a free-for-all in wages and working conditions, and the gross accumulation of corporate wealth, start to bite into the middle strata of professionals and skilled industrial workers. The liberal collectivism of social democracy presupposes the continued role of private and unaccountable corporate management in economic decision-making. Liberal collectivism is hostage to the economic success and political compliance of the corporate economy.[9]

Associational socialism is the only possible challenge to corporate capitalism that is compatible with a liberal democratic order. It enhances that order by challenging the rule of centralized big government. It is compatible with the community, ethical and lifestyle pluralism of modern societies, which has shown no tendency to decrease and which threatens to subvert the universalist aims of liberal collectivist welfare by seeking diverse social objectives. Western societies find it difficult to accommodate the demands of social pluralism within the dual hierarchies of corporate capital and centralized states; in consequence they encounter increasing problems of controlling groups and agencies they are forced to marginalize. Associationalism and pluralism, on the contrary, can accommodate such diversity of values and social objectives. They can therefore draw on the support of diverse constituencies without contradiction. The only way traditional socialism can cope with such pluralistic values and diverse objectives is by imagining that they can be accommodated as subaltern 'allies' in a hegemony created by a single social force, a centralized political party claiming to represent 'labour'. In a society where 'labour' has lost this automatic centrality, such a political project is a liability. Associationalism and pluralism, on the contrary, are political objectives that can be shared by social and political forces with quite distinct objectives. Socialists would be part of a project to construct a genuinely pluralist democracy, and one in which the rule of law would be paramount. In such a project they would be tolerated as partners. As the putative masters of a centralized socialist state, they will be feared and opposed by the very forces they condescendingly treat as 'allies'. It is about time socialists abandoned this futile claim to hegemony and took democracy and social pluralism seriously to heart.[10]

6

Can socialism live?

In the 1880s socialism claimed to represent a better future and one that would certainly come to fruition within a century. It offered a new world that would not merely put an end to the obsolete capitalist system and its evils, but would assure plenty, equality and freedom for all mankind. If Marx or Morris could be woken from the slumber of death and shown the world 100 years later, how they would shudder at the sight of modern intellectuals offering Adam Smith and the free market as solutions to the evils of authoritarian socialism and bureaucratic collectivism. Living socialists are no less shaken by the fact that the future is being brazenly stolen from them, that the free market right has appropriated one of socialism's central rhetorical tropes. It is now socialism that is claimed to be an idea whose time is past.

How has this reversal of fortunes come to pass? Can socialists regain the future and once again offer an intellectually powerful and politically credible alternative conception of social organization? Some on the left will say that to ask such questions shows a craven collapse before an imaginary intellectual hegemony of the right. The enemy's apparent success is the result of our own failure of nerve and not of any real exhaustion of socialist political ideas. Certainly, most right-wing theorists are intellectually banal and their economic and social analyses sketchy, sadly lacking in evidence to support their case. But demonstrations of intellectual weakness will not defeat the right, and not merely because it has access to the money and the information media of the powerful. Left-wing intellectuals have repeatedly demonstrated the flaws of Friedman, Hayek, Nozick, et al. The issue, however, is not can we 'answer' the right, as if it were a matter of scoring points in a university seminar. Of course we can answer them. What is less easy to do is to offer answers to our own problems. The right's success is measured not only in its own ideological strength, but in our objective weakness. What we have difficulty in doing is not merely regaining the confidence of the 1880s, but actually being justified in that confidence, because we possess a conception of social organization that will work, that will be better than existing conditions, and that is politically attainable.

In the 1880s, socialism represented the future and it was as yet untried. The nineteenth century was the century of socialism or, rather, of social*isms*, for it offered a vast array of systems, differing as much from one another as they did from the opposing liberal and free-market doctrines: Saint Simon, Fourier, Owen, Blanc, Proudhon, Lassalle, Marx and Engels, Morris, Bellamy and the Webbs offered different visions of the future and different ways of getting there. Out of this vast mass of ideological possibilities only two forms of socialism became historical actualities: the parliamentary and reformist socialism of the Western European labour movements and the revolutionary and authoritarian Bolshevism of Russia and the underdeveloped countries which followed in its path. In both cases, this was because these forms of socialism attuned themselves to the prevailing conditions and forms of political struggle and these conditions were far from favourable to socialism. It is only by looking at the history of the 'successes' of socialism that we can see why socialism is so hard pressed in Britain today.

In the nineteenth century, the popular-democratic revolutionary tradition inaugurated by the French Revolution was everywhere defeated and contained. Bloodily suppressed in the Paris Commune of 1871, more quietly contained by the special constables drawn from the respectable classes in the case of the Chartist agitation in England, it was given the *coup de grâce* by representative-democratic concessions and by the economic and social modernization of late nineteenth- and early twentieth-century Europe. Socialism was the successor to this tradition, and it had to adapt to changed conditions of political and social struggle or perish. Democratization and ruling-class social engineering sought to domesticate and incorporate the new working classes: extension of the franchise, educational reforms, public health measures, unemployment benefits and social insurance – all were intended both to mitigate the harshness of capitalism and to give the worker a place in society as a citizen. The socialists who succeeded in Western Europe took account of this change and exploited the new institutions of the political party and the trade union.

The German Social Democrats and the British Labour Party were the two most successful in this respect. Both combined effective electoral competition with a stable and continuing link with a relatively unified trade union movement. The German party (the SPD) succeeded in dominating the German socialist movement not because it subscribed to the ideas of Marx and Engels, but because it did not abstain from standing in elections to the Imperial Parliament (the *Reichstag*). The Imperial constitution provided for universal manhood suffrage and in a country with a rapidly urbanized, young and growing working class. The SPD was competing in a new political system for the votes of a newly enfranchised group without established political allegiances.

Marx and Engels increasingly placed their hopes for revolutionary socialist change in universal suffrage and proletarianization. They believed that the working class would become the immense majority of the population and of the electorate as full industrialization developed and eliminated the traditional middle strata of petty traders, artisans and peasants. Such a hope was futile, as one of their brightest disciples, Eduard Bernstein, showed.[1] He argued that the working class could never become so large a proportion of the population and so unified in its attitudes and interests that a revolutionary socialist party would enjoy an unchallengable majority of the popular vote. Yet the legitimacy required to overwhelm the ruling powers and build socialism through parliamentary means required just such a mandate. This built-in limit to electoral victory meant that even the most successful socialist parties had to accept lesser goals if they were to remain in the parliamentary system. If they left it and followed an insurrectionary course, they would be marginalized, contained and destroyed. Bernstein argued that radical reforms were possible on the basis of parliamentary government, but not revolutionary socialism. He became a political leper because he had exposed the political illusions of both parliamentary and insurrectionary socialists. He was right, the parliamentary socialists were forced on to a reformist course, and the German insurrectionary socialists were destroyed in 1918 – in a bitter irony by a nominally socialist government using neo-fascist mercenaries and brutalized ex-soldiers of the *Freikorps*.

Both the SPD and the Labour Party (in its 1918 Clause 4) retained the ultimate formal aim of replacing private capitalist production and distribution by socialism, but both in practice settled for programmes of reform: workers' rights, welfare provision and limited nationalizations. Socialism had become, as Bernstein said, an ever-receding goal and the movement for reform the actuality of parliamentary socialist practice. Socialist reformism in Britain gradually changed into social democracy (in the modern sense) with the advent of Keynesian economics and then with the unexpected post-1945 boom. The 1950s proclaimed the obsolescence and death of revolutionary socialism. C. A. R. Crosland in *The Future of Socialism* (1956) redefined socialism to match the new conditions. National economic management would ensure sustained economic growth on the basis of private capitalist production. This growth would in turn provide the resources for an adequate social welfare system and for the attainment of genuine equality of opportunity. The German SPD changed its programme at its 1959 Bad Godesburg congress, subscribing fully and in principle to social democracy. The Labour Party, despite Gaitskell's efforts, retained what had become the illusions of Clause 4, but in practice adopted a reduced version of Crosland's objectives.

If the 1950s were marked by the claimed death of revolutionary socialism, the 1980s were marked in Britain by a denial from the right of even the feasibility or legitimacy of social democracy. When Mrs Thatcher said in the run-up to the 1987 General Election that a third term would enable her to bury socialism, she meant by that word the Labour Party and Crosland's vision.

Crosland was willing to put up with private capitalist production, because it delivered the goods and because it thereby avoided the defects of authoritarian central planning. When private capitalist production has failed to deliver the goods, as it has in Britain since the 1970s, then it has not been private enterprise and the market system that have been put in question, but social democracy. Social democracy depended on three conditions for its intellectual hegemony and the absence of political challenges to it. First, sustained growth in world trade and national economic growth, which made the task of national macro-economic management relatively easy. Secondly, full employment, which limited the demands placed on the welfare and redistributive apparatus and which limited tax demands on the incomes of the employed. Thirdly, the effectiveness of the private management of production and investment, which limited the role of government to adjusting macro-economic aggregates. The 1973 oil-price shock and the resultant combination of rapid inflation and depression in trade made the job of social democrats everywhere more difficult. It made traditional demand management appear inadequate and thereby gave apparent legitimacy to monetarist deflationary doctrines and supply-side attempts to restore demand through the decisions of private economic agents, rather than inflationary government action. Likewise, economic depression and rising unemployment placed strains on the welfare system and began to reveal its costs. Social democracy has survived the crisis elsewhere in the world and has made successful political comebacks, as in Sweden.

But Britain is the 'weak link' of social democracy. This is because added to the general problems of economic management caused by stagflation and unemployment has been the growing failure of private manufacturing industry to invest and effectively to compete. Britain's economic decline has shifted from a problem of relative failure, that is, to hold a stable share of world trade, to an almost catastrophic failure to maintain a reasonable share of domestic markets, and to widespread deindustrialization[2]

Labour came to office in 1964 pledged to modernize British industry and halt its decline. Having ruled during 1964–70 and 1974–9 it can hardly avoid a share of the blame. In fact Labour never possessed either the political will or the policy means to correct this decline. Its version of social democracy presupposed an economic and social environment which permitted it to function, but that environment was beyond its own governmental mechanisms of control. It abandoned the National Plan, relinquishing any attempt to get firms to plan for sustained investment-led growth. It failed to sustain incomes policies and thereby adjust incomes to productivity growth or attain a favourable balance between consumption and investment. Whatever might have happened, if such measures had succeeded, the government could not have substituted itself for the product and marketing decisions of British managers, and across a broad range of industries these have proved to be disastrous. Since the early 1960s the prospects for a purely *national* social democratic strategy have weakened. The internationalization of trade in manufacture, the linking of world money and equity markets has radically reduced the autonomy of national economic management and with it the security of the national economic base. Advanced industrial countries must match up to the conditions of international competition in manufactures if their industrial bases are to survive. Social democracy thus depends on the skill and commitment of national capitalist managements; their failure undermines the whole strategy.

In Britain the challenge to social democracy posed by changing economic conditions was mounted from the right. Short-sighted, incompetent and inefficient managers escaped virtually scot-free. The unions were blamed for industrial decline, as was, by implication, the party that represented them. Whatever the justice of this accusation, there can be no doubt as to its propaganda success. In 1978–9 Labour lost its last trump card, the ability to control union wage demands, in the 'Winter of Discontent'. The Conservatives also offered tax cuts, especially attractive to manual workers, for whom the tax burden had appeared to grow steadily and rapidly under Labour.

Mrs Thatcher began as a stern monetarist, but rapidly became a Micawberite opportunist, peddling an even tawdrier version of 'you've never had it so good'. Her Government has been able to offer private sector employees in work continued rising real wages. She has continued to fulfil the 1960s expectations for a steady and rising standard of living. That this has been achieved by a selective but highly restrictive *de facto* incomes policy in the public sector, at the expense of adequate provision for the poor and unemployed, because of the balance of payments bonus of North Sea oil, and by asset-stripping the nationalized industries to sustain payments on current account and keep taxes down is widely known and greeted with a quite shocking degree of indiffference. The affluent like their affluence today, and have been educated to no longer worry about tomorrow, many affluent manual workers included.

The genuine social democratic alternative to this policy of 'damn tomorrow' is daunting. In the 1930s Keynesian alternative economic policies would have permitted all sections of the population to benefit. Putting unused capacity to work through stimulating effective demand did not strike at the affluent and the employed in order to help the unemployed. Rigidity of economic and political doctrine prevented their adoption then, economic circumstances prevent their use now.

The alternative programme now implies control to private-sector wages to check inflation and to keep incomes in line with growth in productivity, rising taxes for the well-to-do and a cut in their subsidies (like mortgage interest relief, company cars, etc.), the switching of resources from consumption to investment, and, therefore, a short-term fall in living standards for the affluent and employed. The alternative benefits low-paid workers and the unemployed and it commits resources to investment in a future which may not work anyway. British managers can botch it again. The affluent in Britain have learned and remembered only one thing from the Keynesian era, Keynes's quip 'in the long-run we are all dead.'

Restoring social democracy, the reformist and far from revolutionary task of rehabilitating and humanizing capitalism, involves a daunting challenge in the sick man of the OECD. It involves in particular the affluent making sacrifices for people they despise far more than they fear, the poor and the unemployed. It also involves a complex programme of industrial renewal that may well fail, that the state lacks the competence to carry out, and that the cynical and cautious managers of private industry have no confidence in. The sacrifices are not vast, they involve no risk to life or limb, no hunger or cold, simply the ending of a consumption bonanza, sponsored by the tax man and at the expense of the poor. But why make them when you don't believe in the future? Spend the oil money on foreign manufactures while it lasts and throw another worker on the dole.

A measure of the prevailing mood is how far the Labour Party has been from proposing a fully social-democratic, let alone a socialist, programme. Certainly, it has talked about freedom and fairness, the need for greater equality, for industrial renewal and so on. But its actual policy proposals in the 1987 Election were very limited. Its economic and social policies fell far short of the radical programme of social reconstruction the situation demanded. Its welfare proposals are less radical than those Dick Taverne's commission proposed to the SDP. It proposed a limited and cautious assault on unemployment, which would still leave millions on the dole. Its industrial policy was and still remains vague. It was too scared to openly confront the unions with the need for an incomes policy. And yet Labour still lost the Election. Electoral politics impose their own conditions and parties cannot escape them. To criticize the Labour leadership for 'betrayal' and so on is childish. Labour is trapped in a form of political competition not of its making and which it cannot abandon.

Britain is a cautionary tale of the economic and political limits of social democracy. But reformism and social democracy were imposed on Western socialist parties by the conditions of political competition set by parliamentary democracy. Revolutionary socialism was never a viable alternative in the West and never commanded more than a tiny fraction of the socialist Western movements. Elsewhere political conditions were different, but no less compelling. Some socialists in the West initially and naively hailed the October Revolution of 1917 as an unexpected triumph for socialism. But it was not socialism that had triumphed in Russia, but revolution. Lenin said as much himself, in 1918, and the failure to export revolution to the West further threatened socialism in the East. For all the subsequent propaganda drivel about the 'Workers' Fatherland', the Soviet Union was a backward country hijacked by a small, armed elite of revolutionaries. The Mensheviks had quite rightly insisted upon the problems of socializing an economically backward country in which the development of capitalist industry had hardly begun. Committed to orthodox Marxism, they wished to cooperate with the bourgeois classes in the development of capitalism and democracy in order to provide an objective basis for socialism. Actually they would probably have been silenced by a rightist military *coup d'état*. The Socialist Revolutionaries remained closely committed to the freedom and prosperity of the people they claimed to represent, the peasantry, and, rightly, feared the authoritarianism of the Bolsheviks.

Rapid socialization in the Soviet Union was carried through against the advice of virtually every intelligent Marxist and socialist. Rosa Luxemburg and Karl Kautsky probably only ever agreed about one thing in all their lives and that was that the Bolshevik *putsch* involved a degree of authoritarianism that must cripple socialism.[3] Lenin and Bukharin rapidly changed their ideas and came to see that the pace of socialist social change must be adjusted to what the peasantry could accept, tolerate and pay for. The majority of Marxists and socialists had traditionally envisaged socialism as empowering the people and giving them greater freedom in the course of building socialism. Lenin and Trotsky, for all their ruthlessness, genuinely subscribed to this belief. Stalin and the new Party cadres simply ignored this fundamental assumption and worked on the contrary basis that the pace of social change was governed only by the coercive power of the state and that the direction of change was dictated by the needs of the state and not of the people. The Russian peasantry were bled dry to build a centralized

system of 'planned' heavy industry geared towards defence and the
further expansion of heavy industry. The results we all know, and they
stand as the greatest blow that socialism has ever received.

The 'final solution' destroyed Nazism as a political idea; no one but a
psychopath, a moral leper or a fool would ever seek to endorse Hitler
and Nazism now. Stalinism represented an almost comparable barbarism and like Nazism it too slew millions of innocent victims.[4] Popper,
Hayek and all the lesser anti-totalitarians and anti-central planners
would have nothing sufficient to match their caricature of socialism if
Stalin had not existed. It is all very well to say that Stalinism is only a
caricature of socialism and that the true socialist tradition condemns
Stalin too. 'True socialism' does not exist; the Soviet Union does.

The Soviet system has never fully recovered from Stalin. Stalin was
not a god. He was responsible certainly for all the evil done in his name,
but not the author of all of it. He was merely the leader of the ruthless
and ignorant stratum of new cadres, who outlived him to become the
rulers of the Soviet system. Soviet agriculture was virtually wrecked by
the trauma of collectivization.[5] Soviet manufacturing was trapped
within a rigid structure dominated by heavy industry, given technologies
and central ministerial control. Politics after Stalin slowly retreated
from police state paranoia and the Gulag, but it changed into a system
of collective leadership, buggin's turn and bureaucratic normalcy. A
rule by old men paralysed by caution was perhaps inevitable in the
post-Stalin era. Change and reform were limited because they implied
open political conflict about what to do and the threat of the return of
factional struggles. Nikita Kruschshev, who both challenged the legacy
of Stalinism and attempted reform, was sacked and replaced by the
geriatric immobilism of Brezhnev and his cronies for this very reason.
Mr Gorbachev's regime has barely begun the clearing of a mess that
makes the Augean stables look like an operating theatre. Economic
modernization, solving the productivity problems and eliminating corruption all imply very radical economic reforms and greater democratization. The Soviet elite may well find this process intolerable and stop
it. If they do not, and if the Soviet Union does liberalize and democratize, the result may be to shatter one of the greatest obstacles to
socialism in the West.[6]

But that has yet to happen. Modern Soviet society offers no image of
a better future to the affluent, educated and successful in the West, and
its past offers a grisly vision to the Third World of the costs of 'socialist
primary accumulation'. The Soviet Union has fallen steadily behind the
West in technological development. In the early 1960s, when Kruschshev threatened to 'bury' the West by a process of peaceful coexistence, the relevant economic competition still looked to be a matter of
output of basic products like coal, steel, cement, etc. In the 1980s, the

Soviets lag massively in information and electronic technologies, in chemicals and synthetic products, in sophisticated machine tools and in manufactured consumer durables. The Soviet Union lags behind because it has been unable to offer its highly educated engineers, designers and technicians the autonomy to innovate and work without central direction, and because of the overwhelming consumption of Research and Development effort and advanced technology by the military. To most Westereners, far from offering a better future, it looks like an austere replay of the early 1950s. The Soviet Union's past has not disappeared either. Stalinism was no aberration but a perpetual threat in conditions of the violent seizure of a power by a small revolutionary elite in a backward country. If the consequences of centralized authoritarian state structures imposing forced-march social change on Third World countries needed spelling out after Stalinism, then the Pol Pot regime in Cambodia offered the worst possible lesson.

Parliamentarianism limited the goals of democratic socialism. Authoritarian revolutionary socialism embraced radical goals but in conditions where their realization implied both widespread brutality and an economic system unable to engage in peaceful competition with the West and win. Democratic socialism in the West has been further limited and politically contained by the spectre of authoritarian socialism. The routes politically available to socialist parties have proved problematic for socialism. Social democracy is only as strong as the capacity of private industry to compete in internationalized markets: this is its weakest link and one that undermines the whole chain of welfare provision and national economic management if it goes. Soviet-style socialism is so unpopular that, wherever there is minimal political freedom and open elections, parties proposing radical socialization and centralized economic planning are confined to the wilderness. The hireling publicists and the client intellectuals of the right hardly have to lie or to exaggerate to criticize socialism. Conditions we did not choose and could not avoid have made it all-too-easy to present the future of socialism as an inefficient and ramshackle welfare collectivism or as a pile of skulls.

Politics abhors a vacuum. It is idle for socialist critics to condemn reformism and Stalinism as 'betrayals' of socialism. Democratic socialists *had* to shelve radical socialism as the price of political success in the West, and the working classes supported them with their votes in doing so. Socialists in power offered needed reforms which protected trade unionists, fed and clothed poor children, and so on. Socialists in power were not making socialism, but they *were* helping the people.

Different but equally acute dilemmas of political necessity faced the revolutionary socialists. Should then the Winter Palace not have been stormed? We know Stalinism is not an exception, but an ever-possible consequence of the construction of a revolutionary centralized state in a backward country. The new political elite has risen to power by ruthless and undemocratic means. It is neither checked by traditional social forces, which it crushes, nor possessed of the values and scruples that effective democratic politics enforces, and thus it cannot preserve democracy and openness even within the elite itself. But if this is true of the revolutionaries, it is also true of their enemies. Revolutionary barbarism emerges from reciprocal action with and ruthless struggle against reactionary authoritarianism. Lenin said in the summer of 1917 that the revolution must be completed or it would be destroyed; it could not stand still because its enemies would recover. Hence the primitive either/or, a stark choice between either a Bolshevik or a reactionary *coup d'etat*. Stalinism is the risk of revolutionary socialism, but it is not the inevitable result. There are degrees of authoritarian socialism. Revolutionaries cannot claim to be ignorant of the risk but revolutions are made nonetheless. Brutal and dictatorial rightist regimes cannot simply be endured. To draw the lesson from Stalin or Pol Pot that the left in the Third World should not struggle to overthrow the Somozas or resist the Pinochets of this earth would be nothing less than absurd.

I can imagine many socialists reading this with mounting fury. 'Has the man nothing good to say about socialism?' 'Why doesn't he attack the critics of socialism rather than join them?' My point, however, has not been to answer the critics of socialism, or even to listen to them, but to look as objectively as possible at what has been wrong with socialism. If masses of people reject socialism, not just the rich or the intellectuals, but the sort of ordinary people socialists must convince if they are ever to succeed, then there must be a good reason. Ignore the vapourizings about right-wing and capitalist ideologies having deluded the people. The people are not complete fools. Ignore the fairy stories of 'betrayal'. If the socialist movement had bred nothing but traitors as its leaders for a hundred years, then the true socialists must have been worthless incompetents if they could not compete with them. If we do not honestly face our own problems, then we are like children who blame others for their own acts.

Anyone who imagines that the prospects for electoral success of a radical socialist party in Britain or Western Europe are good, must be a fool. Even if such a party were to get a narrow majority of the electorate (the magic 51 per cent) the strains resulting from an attempt at building socialism quickly by legal means would tear the parliamentary democratic framework apart. The 'veto group' against socialism is a large one and is not confined to a minority of wealthy bourgeois. That group will ruthlessly resist and try to destroy a legal socialist government, and if it fails to do so will solicit the help of foreign allies.

Why not, then, abandon socialism? Because socialism is not only a narrowly pragmatic political enterprise, but it is also based on certain fundamental principles about how society should be organized and how people are to be treated in it. Socialists favour cooperation and mutual assistance over competition, the greatest measure of equality of condition attainable between individuals, the economic autonomy rather than the subordination to management or owner of the worker, and the highest amount of democratic self-government and freedom of expression attainable. These principles rather than any specific institutional arrangements, like central planning, or state welfare, are what is at the heart of the socialist enterprise. It is in terms of these principles that the socialist critique of capitalism is correct. A society dominated by private production for profit on the market, without institutional amelioration and political constraint, generates gross inequality, periodic crises and mass unemployment, misuse of resources and the disregarding of the unmet needs of the poor, and the subordination and insecurity of the worker. A pure free-market capitalism is socially unsustainable and for this reason most capitalist regimes have either embraced social democracy or tried to steal its clothes by conservative social engineering.

Socialism is difficult to attain precisely because its principles are so demanding and are not reducible to technical formulae of attainable institutional reform. Socialism, because it is based on certain fundamental principles and these are concerned with specific forms of social organization, encounters problems most ethical and ideological systems can avoid. Because it evaluates forms of social organization, it cannot be indifferent to the institutional practicality of its ideas. It is interested in social outcomes and, therefore, the measures proposed to attain them must actually work. Socialism is not of an ethic of personal conduct, that can advocate retreat from the world, and can condemn it as evil. At the same time socialist principles transcend any given set of institutional arrangements, there is no one given and best form of cooperation for example. Principles remain values; they assess states of affairs and are not given in descriptions of states of affairs.

Two main errors tend to arise from this complex relationship between principles, institutions and outcomes. One is utopianism, that is, deriving an ideal society from one's principles, picturing its institutions without reference to their feasibility or the availability of a path to their attainment. What is wrong with utopianism is not the imagining of a better world, we all must do that, but treating what is politically unattainable as a political programme. The other is to fetishize certain given institutions as though they were the essence of socialism, such as central planning, or, on the contrary, to anathematize others as if they were alien to socialism in principle, such s a plurality of political parties competing in democratic elections. The fit between principles and institutions is a complex and open one. Socialisms will differ with differing political and institutional circumstances, and socialisms will differ as systems of ideas because of the different weight given to different component principles.

Curiously, the rightist ideas which claim to snatch the future from socialism are utopian in the worst sense. The libertarian right projects an idealized vision of capitalism on to the complex institutional amalgam which is the present, and then argues this ideal state would solve all our major social problems. They create a ludicrous picture of a purely competitive free-market capitalism in which all economic problems solve themselves by automatic equilibration and in which individuals enjoy the freedom to use their talents and receive rewards proportionate to their ability, industry and willingness to take risks. This 'true' capitalism is as much an illusion as the worst kinds of utopian socialism. The world cannot be made safe for the free market unless the *actual* institutions of capitalism, and the big corporations in particular, are destroyed. Free-market ideologues are the Trotskyists of the right, telling us we could have a perfect capitalism if only reality didn't prove too complex. Once one moves away from this true capitalist fairyland into a world of oligopoly, market imperfections and market failure, externalities and so on, then the 'market' enjoys no special privileges. There are mark*ets*. Market systems may prove the most efficient for some goods and services, even in a thoroughly socialized system, and other forms of distribution prove necessary for others. The libertarian right identify the market with freedom; freedom of choice for consumers, free access to public and perfect information. As an information system the market allows the optimal pattern of choices with the minimum of constraint and administrative intervention.

The market is thus counterposed to bureaucratic collectivism, consumer sovereignty to the administrative decisions of officials. Administered activities confer power on the administrators and subordinate those subject to administration. But it is a perfect market system which is counterposed to the flawed actuality of bureaucratic collectivist welfare and state administered corporate capitalism. Only on certain improbable assumptions – that the free market system maximizes welfare, that in it there is no large group of persons denied essential goods and services because they cannot afford to pay for them, that there is no large number of continuing unemployed unable to support themselves, that externalities can be coped with without excessive state intervention, etc., etc. – can the contrast make any sense. One should not be mesmerized by such drivel. It has gained credence because of the political slippage of social democracy in the post-1973 economic crisis and because the rhetoric of liberty and freedom, its anti-collectivism and anti-bureaucratism, however ludicrous the substance, does strike a popular chord.

Modern societies are dominated by big government, by large-scale bureaucratic organization, and that government is subject to little public accountability. Reformist socialism has promoted big government and extended the scope of state action. In a sense, therefore, the right has a genuine target when it identifies socialism with bureaucratic collectivism. But big government came into existence both to assist and to constrain and control big business. It is bureaucratic collectivism and corporate capitalism which form a couple. This the right simply ignores. It proposes to weaken public regulation and collective welfare provision whilst leaving the powers of corporate capital untouched. A truly 'free' market implies an unparalleled set of interventions by the state to eliminate corporate capital and all its inherent advantages, and also to protect home competitive markets from unfair foreign corporate competition. Plainly this is not envisaged. The libertarian right in practice do not give as much emphasis to restricting the powers of corporations as they do to restricting the power of organized labour.

Socialism is by no means committed to the institutions that social democracy has helped to create in its long semi-partnership and semi-struggle with big government and big business. Socialism once predominantly stood for freedom, self-action and autonomy on the part of the working people and not for collectivist centralization and undemocratic bureaucracy. Socialism has emphasized freedom, but it has also stood for equality, mutuality and cooperation. This combination of principles which are at the heart of the socialist enterprise offers the best answer to the libertarian siren song of the right. Socialism has offered a set of principles for a society, a group of people bound by genuine ties and sharing common values. The free-market right seek to counter that with what is in fact an antagonistic ant-heap, where the highest aims and the most sacred principles boil down to the imperative and right to pile one dollar on top of another. Free-market liberalism stresses self-action but in a wholly individualistic, one-sided and materialistic way. The problem is that the socialism which most clearly and genuinely sought to combine freedom *and* cooperation, that of Proudhon or Morris, to cite two of its exemplars, was highly utopian in its vision of social organization and offered no obvious route to its political attainment.

Proudhon's socialism, for example, simply could not exist in a world of mass political parties, large-scale corporate enterprises, internationalized and rapidly changing technology, ruthless international economic competition and centralized and militarized state power. Social democracy could. Its electoral machine got in the votes. It compromised with nationalism and helped governments to fight wars by ensuring the active and intelligent support of the working classes – for the price of social reforms. It thrived on big government, bending it to its own ends when in office and further extending governmental administrative power by its own reforms. It was a socialism which fitted the institutions of the modern world: bureaucracy, the political party, the nation state, administered mass welfare and large-scale emergency war planning. It helped to shape these institutions and it exploited them to its own purposes. They were not socialist institutions, but they could be used by social democrats to further the cause of social reform. Proudhon's socialism or the English Guild Socialism of G. D. H. Cole supposed a world without competitors, struggle and war: political enemies who must be fought with the means *they* chose, not those one would prefer; foreign powers who threaten domination; and large-scale corporate enterprises which can afford to ruin small cooperatives who compete with them. All these threats spell the death of mutuality, cooperation, democracy and self-action. Socialism has been right in what it said about capitalism, right in offering an opposed version of a society that combined freedom and cooperation, but quite unable to convey that radical vision of post-capitalist society into practice.[7]

But we have seen that in Britain the weakest link of social democracy has broken and it no longer appears the evidently practical alternative to impractical and utopian socialism. A commitment to social democratic social reconstruction in Britain implies a shift in attitudes, a willingness to cooperate and make sacrifices that takes it far beyond the outlook shared by left and right in the post-War consensus. We can no longer defer distributional issues by means of full employment and economic growth and we can no longer rely on the private decisions of company managers and investment markets to assure the manufacturing base for growth. In this respect we have reached a watershed in the relationship between social democracy and socialism. The present short-run prosperity for some economic policies simply cannot last much longer. In the 1990s the contribition of domestic oil production to the balance of payments will begin to taper off radically and the effects of under-investment in British industry will begin to bite as never before. Britain will then be presented with a stark choice between a solution which manages the resulting austerity policies through an attempt to share sacrifices and prevent them falling hardest on the poor and the weak, and one which promotes greater inequality, prosperity for even fewer, and which to sustain its policies relies on increasing political authoritarianism.

The socialism/social democracy which responds to this challenge cannot simply re-run the institutional mechanisms of the post-1945 boom, nor can it convert Britain into a very down-market version of Eastern Europe. The latter would be a 'planned' and rationed seige economy isolated from the rest of the world by tariff barriers behind which inefficient and low-productivity industries survive in the absence of competition and dump on consumers whatever they make. A socialism to manage the hard problems of economic failure cannot be a puritanical and authoritarian socialism. Austerity measures may be required, but the core of socialist doctrine cannot be austerity, levelling, rationing and official orders. That is simply to repeat the caricatures of the right. Socialists must draw on the complex resources of the socialist tradition to offer a socialism appropriate to the times. In particular, we must both learn from the appeal of and be able to exploit the contradictions in the anti-authoritarian rhetoric of the free-marketeers. The right assure us that socialism means shortages, state controls and police supervision. Too much in the past of socialism makes that sufficiently true that we cannot dismiss it as an illusion. The answer is a genuinely libertarian socialism. If anything will threaten the right, it is a socialism which places freedom and autonomy first, and because it does so, does not seek to build socialism at the sacrifice of those values.

The contradiction between the economic liberalism of the right and genuine political liberalism has become glaring. The free-market vision is flawed as a doctrine of *political* freedom. *Laissez faire* can only survive in the face of the market system's failure to deliver an adequate outcome for welfare if the losers are denied effective access to political power and can be prevented from modifying the system to their benefit. Mrs Thatcher told us in her 1987 New Year message that socialism is 'alien to our British character.' She thereby revealed just how little commitment to pluralism modern Conservatism has. It will tolerate but one scale of values, its own, and one principle of social organization, the free market. Mrs Thatcher claims to be committed to 'democracy'. But it is democracy in the limited sense of periodic elections to select which party manages a basically authoritarian, hierarchical and centralized form of government administration. That government exists in her mind to police society to make it fit for the market system. All the more obvious then is the need to destroy socialism, to restrict the competition for political power to those Mrs Thatcher feels safe enough to be defeated by.

The precondition for a genuine liberal democracy is political and social pluralism, that is, a society based on a degree of tolerance of one's opponents, and not on relentless antagonism and denial of those opponents' legitimacy. No parliamentary system can long survive in which the major parties and interests view their competitors in elections as outright enemies. Democracy rests on more than periodic elections and electoral competition. In the absence of genuine pluralism, democracy can hasten its downfall, as the example of the Weimar Republic shows. A complex pluralistic society with differing sets of values, with diffused and decentralized power, and powerful non-state associations is the basis for a genuine democracy. Here authentic political liberalism and libertarian socialism meet in arguing for and defending a central proposition: that democracy is not merely a matter of individual rights, but of the organization of social affairs by associations freely formed of citizens. Such a democratic society is much more compatible with an associational socialism like that of Proudhon, Morris or the early Cole than it is with the illusion of the 'free market'.

We can only defeat the equation of socialism with bureaucratic collectivism and authoritarianism if we embrace pluralism and associationalism fully. If, that is, we accept a society with diverse forms of organization and composed of groups with differing values. If socialists offer in response to Mrs Thatcher's anti-pluralism an equally authoritarian vision of 'smashing capitalism', then they will remain in the wilderness. Socialists must build on the pluralistic elements in society by pluralizing the state. Socialists must commit themselves to reducing and eliminating the powers and functions of centralized and bureaucratic big government, transferring as many of them as possible to independent associations and cooperative bodies. These bodies must be democratically self-governing and regulated by law, and they should receive a share of the public revenue where necessary to carry out their tasks. Socialists must also commit themselves to democratizing and associationalizing large-scale corporate enterprises as far as possible, to promoting both self-management and associational ownership (in the form, for example, of a trust representing various interests). Eliminating big government and leaving the big corporation intact would, of course, lead to the unaccountable and authoritarian power of private government gaining ever-greater scope for action.

The free-market right in practice tolerate powerful private corporations. But even in their formal doctrines the concept of freedom is treated in a wholly one-sided way. The market eliminates authoritarian power because when perfectly competitive it guarantees consumer sovereignty, its outcomes are then the aggregate of individual's free decisions. It requires, however, a public power that can gurantee that freedom. The state must be a guarantor of economic freedom and sufficiently impervious to any pressure to weaken that freedom. If the free-market state is a democracy, it can only be so on the basis of the constitutional inviolability of the individual rights necessary to the market system. The market system aggregates consumers' preferences, and its democracy aggregates citizens' votes; individual choice is supreme, provided no 'imperfections' enter into economics or politics. Associations and political organizations are imperfections in this view. They imply the organized pursuit of interest. They threaten the free-market public power. That power can only appear neutral, can only be 'fair', if it deals only with individuals and those individuals accept the outcomes of the market. Outside a perfect world of perfect competition in which the losers accept the judgement of the market, this political vision is pernicious. The free-market system leads its proponents to oppose all associations other than the neutral state. Extreme economic liberalism is a capitalistic Jacobinism. But self-action and freedom, the foundations of democracy, imply not atomized but associated individuals. In the actual world of differing economic and political interests, a plurality of active associations helps to sustain processes of bargaining and political competition which prevent the dominance of any one group in political power.

If socialism is to revive its cooperative and associational side, and if it is to find political allies who are not socialists but are willing to trust us, then socialism must embrace pluralism fully. A pluralist state, in which power is diffused and dispersed, is compatible with an associational and cooperative socialism that is willing to build by its own efforts and organizational activity, but is also compatible with other social projects and social groups that are willing to build likewise. Socialism will certainly have no future for certain if it preaches a singular future, in which there is room only for socialists.[8] Our present system of electoral competition to control centralized big government means that whichever party holds state power has the potential to determine how others shall live. Socialists have been feared for this reason, and revolutionary socialists always defeated at the polls. It is for exactly the same reason that socialists should now strive as hard as possible to defeat Mrs Thatcher and find as many allies as possible in doing so. But our opposition to the authoritarianism of modern Conservatism is only credible to the extent that people come to believe that socialists do not also seek to exploit and extend state power. If we still aim to construct a centrally planned economy based on state ownership, our opposition to authoritarianism is cynical and purely self-serving.

Socialism is in no sense committed by its basic values to such institutions as central planning and bureaucratically managed state ownership. Indeed, it should be opposed to them because they threaten freedom. Even if a centrally planned economy could be made technically efficient, it is incompatible in principle with a pluralistic and democratic society. Centrally planned production requires the centralizing of decision-making and the information flows necessary to it. A central economic planning apparatus which worked by consent in a society of some complexity and with organized differing interests would find it virtually impossible to incorporate the various competing demands into a single plan. Such a society presupposes bargaining rather than planning. A centrally planned society can be democratic only if the planners are confronted with a homogeneous people without conflicts of interests, if, that is, the plan coincides with the general will. Centralized planning leads to a socialistic Jacobinism. Even on the improbable assumption that the plan has unified democratic assent, its execution has to be authoritative in order to be calculable. The plan can only be certain in effect if all subordinate agents comply with its requirements. A centralized planning process, properly democratic in conception and execution and applying to a complex economy, would quite simply never finish. This is true, however much it was aided by mathematical modelling and sophisticated computers. These techniques also demand highly centralized information, compatible objectives within the plan, and certainty in execution of the plan.

Socialists have to convince the populace that socialism is not exclusively or even primarily about economics. An exclusive concentration on the economic managerial techniques of socialism, whether of central planning or of market socialism, has bedevilled too much socialist theory. Socialism has either been reduced to schemes for economic management in an ideal socialist society, or schemes for the reconstruction of a capitalistic one. No political doctrine can prosper whose basic principles are obscure to ordinary people. A doctrine that requires an esoteric discussion does so because it involves an esotericism of organizational technique. People rightly fear such an esoteric political doctrine. It excludes them twice over: they do not fully understand it, and yet they know it means rule by unaccountable experts.

Socialism must first of all be a political doctrine, and a democratic one. It must be about how to enable the people to conduct their affairs as practically and as freely as possible. A democratic political doctrine can only be practical if it is intelligible to the people and proposes mechanisms they can make use of without special training or elaborate education. Free market libertarianism is attractive, not because it is a complex of technical economics, which it is not, but because of the apparently democratic aspects of its political message. *An associationalist socialism offers an alternative way of performing the political tasks free-marketeers assign to markets.* Those tasks are: to avoid the authoritarianism of administrative allocation, to ensure choice, and to provide an element of competition between agencies offering goods and services. Associational socialism can only do so honestly if it avoids making essentially unjustifiable claims to economic efficiency in the way that central planning ideology and free-market doctrines do. Both of these economic theories have to simplify social relations to meet the needs of their economic information systems, and both exclude an active and associative democracy as a consequence of such simplifications.

If socialists embrace pluralism and associationalism, it must be for real and, therefore, they should be aware of the consequences. An associationalist socialism cannot be 'planned' and it cannot in consequence guarantee the aggregate outcomes of the economic activities of its associations, cooperatives and enterprises. But central planning cannot accomplish this either. Such an associationalist socialism also cannot guarantee equal outcomes in terms of income and welfare between associations or the individuals who make them up. But centralized bureaucratic processes of allocation cannot accomplish this either. What such a pluralistic system can do is to ensure a greater degree of equality of influence in economic and political affairs, and it can prevent accumulations of private wealth or concentrations of authoritarian power.

Socialists must challenge the view attributed to them by the right that they want a levelling equality of outcomes at any price. Marx made it quite clear that such an absolute equality is unattainable and that people do have unequal skills and abilities. What most ordinary people, who are neither dogmatic socialists or convinced capitalists, object to is gross inequality, and not primarily because of the accumulation of wealth itself. A Getty can never consume his fortune, rather it consumes him. Gross inequality is rejected because of the unjustified power over others that it gives to wealthy individuals. People do not worry about equality of incomes as much as they do about access to freedom. A high degree of social autonomy for individuals, that is, the capacity to influence the economic association by which one earns one's livelihood and the capacity to influence public affairs through one's political association, is to be preferred to authoritarian mechanisms which attempt to ensure substantive equality of income and benefits between individuals or households.

An associationalist socialism cannot happen overnight, but it doesn't need to. This is because it need not be the exclusive basis of social organization. It does need a relatively pluralistic and democratic society. Such a society would not exclude associations with non-socialist principles from engaging in economic affairs and welfare provision – religious foundations, for example. It would not exclude conventional firms or private traders. It would, however, impose strong anti-monopoly provisions, which would apply to all types of enterprises, and also limits to personal fortunes. It would accept market exchange but seek to encourage cooperation, mutuality, reciprocity and charity. In the right framework cooperation can compete effectively with materialistic individualism.

The associationalist and cooperative approach has an appeal well beyond socialists. Indeed, it may be more acceptable to many non-socialists than to socialists rigidly committed to the institutions of state socialism. Britain presents a curious paradox, for it is a country that has both a highly centralized and relatively unaccountable government, which controls and directs a great deal of the nation's life, and at the same time one of the most active and vital associational cultures in the Western world. Charities and voluntary associations abound, and they are often efficient providers of vital services, like the RNLI, or run well-managed shops and mail-order operations, like Oxfam. If anyone doubts the skills of freely associated individuals, these examples should suffice to make them pause for thought. If anything it is the Labour Movement's own institutions of mutuality and cooperation that have atrophied, far more than those of the religious congregations or the charities of the concerned middle classes.

But what, you may ask, has this flight of fancy to do with the political problems of the present? Granted the socialism you speak of sounds attractive, but does it not come down to that idle preaching of impractical ideas which is what associationalist socialists have always been beaten into by their more successful competitors? If the gap between socialism and social democracy has narrowed, does this not merely mean that the whole left is about to be finally consigned to the wilderness? The answer to this question is to return to the economic problems that lie ahead in the 1990s. Even if Mrs Thatcher were to win the next election (probably in 1991), Conservative governments cannot go on as hers has up to now. We shall be faced some time in the 1990s with a stark choice between an increasingly authoritarian state that tries to defend fewer and fewer of the affluent in their unjustified privileges and . . . ? Be sure that the 'and' will not be an insurrectionary and revolutionary socialism. However limited the appeal of a right-wing government, it will always have sufficient power to destroy *that*.

The opposition to Mrs Thatcher now or to her successors in the later 1990s poses the same problem. Even if Labour does win the next election, it would be a weak government with very powerful economic and political foes at home and abroad. Labour or a left-inclined coalition can only govern effectively and face the problems posed by economic decline if it can mobilize the largest measure of active non-parliamentary organizational support. That will not be given unless there are good reasons for compliance and to obtain that means the Government getting into and leading a process of organizational bargaining. Getting organized interests to accept and commit themselves to controls and sacrifices will involve both some Governmental coercion and bringing them into the political process.[9]

Starting in this way with a process of social leadership based on bargaining Labour can propose a new, continuing and developing relationship between the state and associations. That relationship will be the exact opposite of the present practices of seeking to enforce the will of government, whatever the opposition. The process would begin with a variant of the corporatism that was halfheartedly attempted in Britain in the 1960s, but which has proved so successful in effectively functioning social democratic states like Sweden. But the process need not stop there. From a limited start such a strategy of social leadership could work towards devolving state power and function to associations, and along with this process work toward broadening the base of and democratizing associations themselves. If the Tories can privatize state-owned firms, we can propose the 'pluralizing' and 'associationalizing' of power and decision-making. Privatization does nothing to change the facts of management control; pluralization would attack precisely this in order to produce a combination of self-management and public accountability.

Rejecting the traditional narrow view of party government, seeking allies, and working with existing organizations to build a policy consensus through bargaining could be the first step in the process of creating a pluralist state and an associationalist society in which cooperative and mutualist socialist groups can flourish. Labour has now dropped a great deal of the baggage of the traditional Labour left. It is clear that extensive re-nationalization, restoring the *status quo anti* for the unions, and large-scale increases in welfare benefits or spending on health and education are now out. But little has come in to replace the institutions of social democracy Mrs Thatcher has set about with such a vengeance. Labour may well fear to be too radical in the face of Mrs Thatcher, but it cannot remain bereft of genuine radicalism for long and survive as a potential party of government.

Associationalist socialism and political pluralism has a long history in Britain and some of the intellectual leaders of the Labour Party such as H. J. Laski and G. D. H. Cole subscribed to it earlier in their careers. Cooperation, mutuality and anti-statism have strong roots in other parties like the Liberals. If Labour committed itself to such ideas, not in a dogmatic or utopian way, but as its guiding principles and as the objectives it worked towards, it would again have the capacity to offer a better future and one which did not cripple it in the political context of the present. People need more than the better management of failure to inspire them as a political objective. It is essential to offer a view of political organization, one which recognizes economic problems and tasks but does not subordinate itself to them. It is a view of how we might live better, even if we do not manage to engineer a British 'economic miracle'. Labour is certainly not promising that there are easy solutions to our problems or that real incomes will rise rapidly, but it is failing to show how a period of enforced economic austerity could nevertheless register political and social gains.

Socialism is not dead. Its enemies would love to kill it, and they have been helped in that task by the objective weaknesses of socialism that have made it unattractive at an instinctive level to so many ordinary people. Our task is to expose our own weaknesses to criticism, learn from our very real failures, and then overcome them.[10] Socialism will not die, because its values are worthy ones and appropriate to the times in which we live. These values need to be expressed in the form of institutions which do not betray them and which are appropriate to these times. The theory of an associationalist socialism in a pluralist state is the doctrine which best secures socialism a future.

7

The problem of sovereignty

Two critical approaches to the liberal theory of
sovereignty: Carl Schmitt's decisionism and 'pluralist'
jurisprudence

The period since 1945 has witnessed a dramatic reduction in both the
variety of intellectual positions and the agenda of issues in Western
political theory and jurisprudence. Political argument has been virtually
reduced to a contest between positions within the context of liberal-
democratic theory. Western Marxism has been the only genuine alternative to these terms of debate, and that in the role of a marginalized and
oppositional outsider. In the 1980s, Marxism and the popular-
democratic radicalism of the 1968 student movement have been all but
eclipsed in public political argument. Even relatively radical democratic
socialists who seek to challenge the economic status quo now take
representative democracy and liberal constitutional government as their
unquestioned points of departure.

There are some genuine benefits which follow from this dramatic
restriction of the terms of political argument. Fascist, Nazi and Stalinist
political ideas are now utterly marginal. It is also the case that the
restriction may be more apparent than real. Political argument in liberal
democratic terms does offer a relatively broad spectrum of positions and
opinions. A context of political theorizing which includes both Hayek
and Rawls is a broad one. But the hegemony of liberal-democratic
political argument tends to obscure the fact that we are thinking in terms
which were already obsolete in the nineteenth century.

Representative democracy, parliamentary government and liberal
constitutionalism are doctrines re-used and re-cycled much as they were
passed on by Constant or Mill or Dicey. Modern big government has
used these doctrines as a means of legitimation and has suffered
precious little restraint in its actions thereby. The 'sovereign power' of

the people's representatives gathered in the legislature has been placed at the service of the executive through enabling legislation. One could elaborate the discrepancies between liberal-democratic governmental doctrine and political practice more or less endlessly. The liberal-democratic view of politics is grossly at variance with our political condition. Conservative liberals like Hayek perceive this and try to persuade us to re-create the social and political conditions of the mid-nineteenth century in an idealized fashion. In fact, they end up as the purely ceremonial intellectual totems for some of the most un-savoury interests and forces of the late twentieth century, interests and forces that are determined to exploit out actually illiberal and undemo-cratic political condition to the full. Radicals are concerned to use a political machinery that they perceive in liberal-democratic terms in order to deliver economic and social reform. They perceive existing democratic institutions as part of the solution and not as the major social problem and object of reform which they are. Conservative liberals, like Hayek, perceive clearly the problems involved in the existence of big government, but only in the context of an archaic view of economic and social relations. They seek to make the world fit for individualist liberalism, rather than to recognize the obsolescence of that political doctrine. Radical liberal-democrats, on the other hand, do not really perceive the problem, in that they seek to extend the scope of government action without devising new means of control and coordina-tion of governmental agencies.

The shock of Nazism and Stalinism scared the vast mass of Western politicians and their electorates into a rigid adherence to liberal democratic doctrines. The agenda of political discussion rigidified to an excessive degree, and it remains rigid. The rise of the New Right has served to reinforce the terms of argument by pitting classical liberalism against democracy, and by pitting the rights of the individual against an economic-interventionist democratically legitimated state. The majority of the theorists of the New Right do not challenge either the sovereignty of the state or the basis of that sovereignty in representative govern-ment. They seek to restrict the functions of the state, whilst at the same time conceiving of it as a sovereign public power able to assure public peace. Even a state restricted in its functions to war, police and justice – if such were possible under modern economic and social conditions – raises the problems involved in liberal-democratic conceptions of sovereignty in an acute form. Conservative liberal theories of rule of law and social-democratic theories of an interventionist social-welfare state alike evade the central questions of how to ensure public accountability and control when faced with modern multiform big government. The former imagine it possible to reduce the problem to nothing by taking the state back to the mid-nineteenth century and the latter, if they really see the problem, duck it with ad hoc palliatives like a Freedom of Information Act.

The terms of debate have not always been so enclosed and enfeebled. In the first three decades of this century, liberal democratic political theory and the notion of popular sovereignty through representative government were widely challenged. This challenge came from supporters of classical Marxism, from labour and administrative syndicalists, from 'pluralists' and Guild Socialists, and from proto-fascists and fascists. Much of this challenge was mere demagogic rhetoric and was made on behalf of doctrines of social organization which were little better than absurd. The anti-liberal criticism of Sorel or Maurras or Mussolini may be telling on occasion, but their alternatives to liberal democracy are poisonous and one can only heave a sigh of relief that they have no place in modern political argument. The same can be said of much of the ultra-leftist and left-Communist political theory in this period. Other arguments are consigned to the garbage heap of political theory at our peril. The two which I shall consider here challenge the liberal-democratic theory of sovereignty in a way that enlightens us about contemporary political conditions and political debates. They are Carl Schmitt's decisionist jurisprudence and the various 'pluralist' theories of the state and law. In regard to the latter, I shall consider the English pluralists G. D. H. Cole, John Neville Figgis and H. J. Laski hardly at all here, and concentrate on the work of Léon Duguit and on the theoretical support to his jurisprudence provided by Émile Durkheim's sociology.[1] The pluralists need no special explanation or apology. They accepted the ideals of liberal democracy even as they disputed its doctrines. Despite their criticism of the defects of liberalism none of them wished for a social order with fewer freedoms for individuals or with less effective control by political bodies over the administration of public affairs.

Carl Schmitt is a more difficult case. Elements of his political theory before the Nazi seizure of power are undoubtedly 'fascist' and he did become a servant of the Nazi state – although like many German ultra-conservatives he came to regret it and lived in a dishonoured political impotence in the later years of the Third Reich. However, Schmitt asks hard questions and he points to aspects of political life too uncomfortable to ignore. If his view of politics is flawed, it permits a striking recognition of some of the defects of liberal-democratic doctrine. Schmitt's analyses are not governed by a concrete political alternative to liberal democracy; hence he seldom sinks to the level of demagogery, special pleading or point scoring. His position has often been regarded as nihilistic, but the very absence of a stable political platform in his work lends to his thought the capacity for a certain kind of objectivity. Schmitt can appreciate at one and the same time the political energy and ruthlessness of Trotsky, the myth-making power of Sorel's syndicalist doctrines and Mussolini's practice, and the nationalist fervour of Pearse and Connolly. He can admire the authoritarian statist conservatism of Donoso Cortes and yet also admire the ruthless anti-statist anarchism of Bakunin.

In part this mobility of judgement stemmed from Schmitt's view of politics as friend–enemy relations; he appreciated those who viewed politics as decisive struggle. This view of politics also led him to change suddenly from contemptuous opposition to Hitler to endorsement of Nazism. If the lack of substantive ethical standards above politics which can be used as a means to judge political conduct is nihilism, then Schmitt was a nihilist. He would join many modern political thinkers, left and right, in this respect. What led Schmitt to make common cause with the Nazis was not his ethical nihilism but, on the contrary, a concern with social order above all else and, like many German conservatives, the disastrous misjudgement that there was no other choice but Hitler or chaos. Schmitt suffered lightly from his flirtation with evil and emerged alive from the chaos into which the Nazis plunged Europe. He merely lost his reputation. Political theorists' works cannot be evaluated on the basis of their personal political judgements alone, however. Marx's life was littered with political errors, as anyone who cares to consult his work on the Eastern Question can confirm. Schmitt's work has value in spite of his errors and his more-than-flirtation with evil; but if we should never for a moment forget or condone or evade the dreadful choice he made.

SCHMITT'S DECISIONISM

The key to this apparently very mobile set of judgements and this chameleon-like capacity to change political position is Schmitt's view of the nature of politics. Schmitt's targets are the liberal constitutional theory of the state and the parliamentarist conception of politics. In such liberal-democratic views the state is subordinated to law, it becomes the executor of purposes determined by a representative legislative assembly. Parliamentarist politics is dominated by 'discussion', by the free deliberation of representatives in the assembly. Schmitt considers nineteenth-century liberal democracy as an anti-political view of politics. Liberalism is a view of politics that is immobilized and rendered impotent by a rule-bound legalism, by a rationalist conception of political debate and the resolution of differences, and by the desire that the individual citizen enjoy a 'private' sphere legally guaranteed and protected against the state.

The political is none of these things; the essence of the political is

THE PROBLEM OF SOVEREIGNTY

struggle. In *The Concept of the Political* Schmitt argues that the *differentia specifica* of the political, which separates it from other activities and spheres of social life, like religion or economics, is friend–enemy relations. The political exists when differences reach the point where groups are placed in a relation of enmity, where each comes to perceive the other as an irreconcilable enemy to be struggled against and if possible defeated. Such relations are specifically political and possess an existential logic that overrides the motives which may have brought groups to this pass. Each group now faces an enemy and must take account of that fact: 'Every religious, moral, economic, ethical, or other antithesis transforms itself into a political one if it is sufficiently strong to group human beings effectively according to friend and enemy' (*The Concept of the Political* (1976), p. 37). The political consists not in war or armed conflict between groups as such, but in relation of enmity which forces groups to struggle one with another, not to compete but to contest not to discuss but to confront. Politics is bound by no law; it is prior to Law.

For Schmitt: 'The concept of the state presupposes the concept of the political' (*Concept of the Political*, p. 19). States arise as a means of continuing, organizing and channelling political struggle. It is political struggle which gives rise to political order; a body involved in friend–enemy relations inevitably becomes political whatever its origin or the origin of the differences leading to enmity. Schmitt says: 'A religious community which wages wars against members of other religious communities or engages in other wars is already more than a religious community; it is a political entity' (*Concept of the Political*, p. 37). Politics arises from the struggle of groups and order is imposed within them to pursue conflict outside them. To view the state as the settled orderly administration of a territory, concerned with the organization of its affairs according to law, is to see only the stabilized results of conflict. It is also to ignore the fact that the state stands in a relation of enmity to other states, that it possesses its territory by means of armed force and, therefore, that on this basis of a monopoly of force it can make claims as to the lawful government of that territory. The pacific, legalistic, liberal-parliamentary bourgeoisie are sitting on a volcano and ignoring the fact. Their world depends on a relative stabilization of the conflicts of religious and socio-economic groups within the state and on the state's capacity to keep at bay potentially hostile states without.

For Hobbes the political state arises from a compact on the part of men to submit to a Sovereign who will put an end to the war of all against all which must otherwise prevail in a state of nature. For Schmitt the political condition is a relation between definite friend–enemy groupings – what internal order there is in these groupings is a consequence of the need to face the enemy; those who are not for the group are against it. Schmitt starts where Hobbes leaves off, with the contest of political societies, with the natural state between organized competing groups or states as one of war. Or rather, it is the *contest* which produces political groups and, therefore, that state of nature.

Faced with a truly 'political' conflict no amount of discussion, compromise or exhortation can settle the issue between friend and enemy. All negotiation and buying-off are merely moments in the conflict. There can be no genuine discussion between enemies because there is nothing in the end for them to agree about. The essence of political action is struggle and the issues in such struggle are simple, the either/or, friend or enemy. Politics, dominated as it is by the either/or, requires *decision* and not discussion. No amount of reflection can change an issue which is so existentially primitive that it precludes it. For Schmitt speeches and motions in assemblies are not contrasted with blood and iron as such, for dithering parliamentarians can cause blood to be shed in plenty, but with the moral force of the decisive decision.

Parliamentarianism and liberalism exist in a particular historical moment between the absolutist state of the seventeenth century and the 'total state' of the twentieth. Parliamentary discussion and a liberal 'private sphere' presupposed the depoliticization of a large area of social, economic and cultural life. The state provided a legally codified order within which social customs, economic competition and religious belief could be pursued freely and without political contest. 'Politics' ceases to be a matter of the state and government in the narrow sense when 'state and society penetrate each other' (*Concept of the Political*, p. 22). The modern total state breaks down the depoliticalization on which such a narrow view of politics could rest:

> Heretofore ostensibly neutral domains – religion, culture, education, the economy – then cease to be neutral . . . Against such neutralisations and depoliticisations of important domains appears the total state, which potentially embraces every domain. This results in the identity of state and society. In such a state . . . everything is at least potentially political, and in referring to the state it is no longer possible to assert for it a specifically political characteristic. (*Concept of the Political*, p. 22)

The areas of political struggle and the agenda of political demands cannot, therefore, be limited. Democracy has conquered liberalism and it does away with the depoliticizations characteristic of rule by a narrow bourgeois stratum insulated from popular demands. Mass politics means a broadening of the agenda to include the affairs of the whole of society – everything is potentially political. Mass politics also threatens the existing forms of constitutional and legal order. The politicization of all domains increases the pressure on the state by multiplying the competing groups and interests demanding action. Once the whole of society becomes political, the function of the liberal framework of laws – the regulating of the 'private sphere' – becomes inadequate. The state, subject as it is to the pressures of mass demands and of industrial interests, must intervene in the economy. The state can no longer confine itself to promulgating universally applicable general laws, but must take specific administrative measures and order the affairs of definite groups. Once the affairs of the whole of society become a matter of political decision, the existing liberal constitutional framework then comes to threaten social order: politics ceases to be a matter of the discussion of individual notables; rather it becomes a contest of organized parties and interests. These parties and interests seek to prevail rather than to achieve reconciliation or the best outcome through discussion and compromise, and hence a weak state bound by law which allows every party and group an 'equal chance' is threatened with dissolution. The total state must be far stronger and less bound in its action by formal legal niceties, if it is to accomplish its tasks and to contain group conflict. The state can only be the main political grouping if it can forestall antagonisms developing to a political level within it. This implies authoritative centres within the state capable of acting on decision and without excessive legal and parliamentary constraint.

Schmitt may be an authoritarian conservative but his diagnosis of the defects of parliamentarism and liberalism is a genuine *analysis* rather than the mere re-statement of value-positions. Schmitt's conception of 'sovereignty' is a challenging one and it forces us to think very carefully about the conjuring trick which is 'law'. Liberalism tries to make the state subject to law. Laws are lawful if properly enacted according to set procedures, hence the 'rule of law'. In much liberal democratic constitutional doctrine the legislature is held to be 'sovereign' and it derives its law-making power from the will of the people expressed through their representatives. The rule of law – the procedures which make laws lawful – depends on some constituting act of sovereignty in which these procedures are set down. Liberalism relies on a constituting political moment in order that the 'sovereignty' implied in democratic legislatures be unable to modify not only specific laws but also law-making processes at will and therefore, convert the 'rule of law' into a merely formal doctrine. If the rule of law is simply the people's will expressed through their representatives then it has no determinate content and the state is no longer substantively bound in its actions by law. Classical liberalism implies a highly conservative version of the rule of law and a sovereignty limited by a constitutive political act that is beyond the reach of normal politics. It is challenged by democracy, which threatens the parliamentary-constitutional regime with a boundless sovereign power which is claimed to come from the 'people'.

What this reveals is that all legal orders and laws have an 'outside', that they rest on a politics which is prior to and is not bound by law. A constitution can only survive if the constituting political act continues to be sustained by some existing political power. The 'people' do not exist except in the claims of that tiny minority – their 'representatives' – which functions as a 'majority' in the chamber of the legislative assembly. The analysis of 'sovereignty' is therefore not a matter of formal constitutional doctrine or essentially hypocritical references to the 'people'; it is a matter of determining which particular agency has the capacity – outside of law – to impose an order which, because it is political, can become legal.

Schmitt cuts through 300 years of political theory and public law doctrine to define sovereignty in a way that renders endless debates about the principles of political obligation or the formal constitutional powers of different bodies idle. He says:

> From a practical or theoretical perspective, it really does not matter whether an abstract scheme advanced to define sovereignty (namely, that sovereignty is the highest power, not a derived power) is acceptable. About an abstract concept there will be no argument . . . What is argued about is the concrete application, and that means who decides in a situation of conflict what constitutes the public interest or interest of the state, public safety and order, *le salut public*, and so on. The exception, which is not codified in the existing legal order, can at best be characterised as a case of extreme peril, a danger to the existence of the state, or the like. But it cannot be circumscribed factually and made to conform to a preformed law. (*Political Theology*, (1985), p. 6)

Brutally put: 'Sovereign is he who decides on the exception' (*Political Theology*, p. 5). The sovereign is a definite agancy capable of making a decision, not a legitimating category (the 'people') or a purely formal definition (plenitude of power, etc., etc.). Sovereignty is *outside* of law, since the actions of the sovereign in the state of exception cannot be bound by laws (necessity has no laws). To claim that this is anti-legal is to ignore the fact that all laws have an outside, that they exist because of a substantiated claim on the part of some agency to be the dominant source of binding rules within a territory. Public law can exist ony because political conditions are stable enough to make it possible. The sovereign (no abstraction but a definite agency) determines the possibility of the rule of law by deciding on the exception: 'For a legal order to make sense, a normal situation must exist, and he is sovereign who definitely decides whether this normal situation actually exists' (*Political Theology*, p. 13). A legal order and constitutionally limited government rest on their antithesis, upon 'unlimited authority, which means the suspension of the entire existing order' (*Political Theology*, p. 12).

Schmitt's view of the foundation of the legal order in a condition so apparently antithetical to it rests on his concept of the political. Political groupings are decisive because they organize friend–enemy relations. It is the political grouping which decides who is friend and who is enemy, what is the condition of enmity, and what to be done about it – these decisions are not legal but political. If a political 'entity exists at all it is always the decisive entity, and it is sovereign in the sense that the decision about the critical situation, even if it is the exception, must always necessarily reside here' (*Concept of the Political*, p. 38).

Schmitt's conception of the state of exception is not nihilistic or anarchistic. On the contrary, Schmitt's thinking is based upon his concept of the political, but it is concerned with the state, with the preservation of legitimate government and with the defence of the stable and lasting institutions of society. He argues that 'exception is different from anarchy and chaos' (*Political Theology*, p. 12), it is an attempt to restore order in a political sense. While the state of exception can know no norms the actions of the sovereign agency within the state must be governed by what is prudent to restore order. Barbaric excess and pure arbitrary power are not Schmitt's object; rather the stabilization of politics such that legal norms can be restored ought to be the aim of the sovereign's actions. Power is limited by a prudent concern for the social order, much like a judge considering individuals' actions under 'normal' legal conditions: in the exception 'order in the juristic sense still prevails even if it is not of the ordinary kind' (*Political Theology*, p. 12). Schmitt may be a relativist with regard to ultimate values in politics but he is a conservative concerned to defend a political framework in which the 'concrete orders' of society can be preserved. Like most extreme conservatives he is all too aware of the paradox that that which ought to endure is actually threatened and demands exceptional efforts in order that it be preserved. Schmitt is thus not a nihilist in the sense that Hermann Rauschning, in *Germany's Revolution of Destruction* (1939) considered the Nazis to be, that they treated all existing social institutions as nothing beside certain idealized entities such as the Führer and the Volk. Schmitt, for all his stress on struggle as the essence of politics and on the state of the exception, does not favour a militarization of politics and society, in which images of struggle and forms of authority as pure command become idolized. The exception is the exception, not the rule – as it is in fascist political imagery.

Just as forms of liberalism abolished politics in discussion and the state in its legal (self) limitations so the fascists and Nazis glorified struggle and arbitrary power into ends in themselves. Schmitt is cautioning against a liberal politics which cannot preserve the social order if its illusions are persisted in, but too often he appears to subscribe in showing how law depends on politics, the norm on the exception, stability on struggle, to the contrary illusions of the fascists. In fact, Schmitt's work can be used as a critique of fascism – and a most powerful critique – precisely because it is but a hair's breadth away from it. Schmitt's ruthless logic in his analysis of the political, the nature of the sovereignty and the exceptional state demonstrates the irrationality of fascism. The exception cannot be made the rule in the total state without reducing society and economy to such a disorder through the political actions of the fascist mass party that the very survival of the state is threatened. The Nazi state sought war as the highest end in politics but conducted its affairs in such a chaotic way that its war-making capacity was undermined and its war aims became fatally boundless.

Schmitt's jurisprudence of the exception modernizes the absolutist doctrines of Bodin and Hobbes. It restores – in the state of exception rather than as the norm – the sovereign as uncommanded commander. For Hobbes, laws were orders given by those with authority – '*autoritas, non veritas, facit legem*'. Confronted with complex systems of procedural limitation in public law, with impersonal, universally valid general rules, and with the formalization and intellectualization of law into a system, Hobbes's views appeared increasingly obsolete – laws were far more complex than orders in their form, and their origin was itself rule-governed. Modern legal positivism and formalism could point to a normal liberal-parliamentary legal order which contradicted Hobbes and they still do. Even in the somewhat modernized form of John Austin, the Hobbesian view of sovereignty is rejected on all sides. It was Schmitt's genius to found his jurisprudence neither on the normal workings of the legal order nor on the formal niceties of constitutional doctrine but on a condition quite alien to them. Schmitt recognizes that 'normality' rests on non-legal, non-constitutional conditions, a certain balance of political forces, a certain capacity of the state to impose order if need be not by its constitutional powers but by the power of weapons. This is true especially of the parliamentary-liberal regime. Its public law requires a stabilization of political conflicts and a considerable power of war and police even to begin to have the slightest chance of functioning at all. Law cannot form a completely rational and itself lawful system, and the analysis of the state must make reference to those agencies which have the capacity to decide on the state of exception and not merely the claim to a formal plenitude of power.

Schmitt claimed, in *Political Theology*, that the concepts of the modern theory of the state are secularized theological concepts. This is obvious in the case of 'sovereignty' where the omnipotent law-giver is a mundane version of an all-powerful God. Schmitt argues that liberalism and parliamentarism correspond to Deist views of God's action through constant and general natural laws. Schmitt's own view is a form of fundamentalism in which the state of the exception plays the same founding role in relation to the state as the miracles of Jesus do in confirming the Gospels' message. The exception shows the legally unlimited capacity of those whose will is decisive within the state. In conventional liberal-democratic doctrine the people are the sovereign whose will is expressed through representatives. Schmitt argues that modern democracy is a form of populism, the people are mobilized by propaganda and organized interests. Such a democracy bases legitimacy upon the people's will. Parliament therefore exists on the suffrance of the parties, propaganda agencies and organized interests that compete for popular 'consent'. When parliamentary forms and the rule of law become inadequate to the political situation they will be dispensed with in the name of the people: 'no other constitutional institution can withstand the sole criterion of the people's will, however it is expressed' (*Political Theology*, p. 15).

Schmitt thus accepts the logic of Max Weber's view of plebiscitarian democracy and the rise of bureaucratic mass parties which utterly destroy the autonomy of the old parliamentary notables. He uses the nineteenth-century Spanish reactionary, Juan Donoso-Cortes, to set the essential dilemma in *Political Theology*, either a boundless democracy of plebiscitarian populism which will carry us wherever it will, to Marxist or fascist domination, or a dictatorship. Schmitt advocates a specific form of dictatorship as an answer to the state of exception – a commissarial dictatorship which acts to stabilize the social order, to preserve the concrete orders in society and to restore the constitution. The dictator has a constitutional office but acts as a decisive political actor, not as a public official performing a legally specified task. The dictator acts in the name of the constitution, but takes such measures as are necessary to preserve order. These measures of constitutional defence are not actually bound by law. Schmitt's doctrine thus involves a paradox, for all its stress on friend–enemy relations and on decisive political action, for its core is the aim of maintaining stability and order. Schmitt's view of law founds it on a political non-law, but not in the interests of lawlessness. Schmitt regards the constitution as subject to the state of exception and the measures necessary in that state, but those measures are designed to preserve constitutional order. Schmitt is a anti-liberal because he contends liberalism cannot cope with real politics. It can only insist on a legal formalism which is useless in the exceptional state. Hence Schmitt argued against the doctrine that all parties should have an 'equal chance' to contend for power. Parties which threatened the existing order and used the constitutionally guaranteed freedoms to challenge the constitution should be subject to rigorous control.

Schmitt's endorsement of Donoso-Cortes's either/or – with dictatorship or anarchy as the choice – is the characteristic element of his thought. For Schmitt the core of politics is 'the exacting moral decision': either/or, friend–enemy. Politics has no logic other than this choice – reasoning, debate, analysis are, strictly speaking, not part of politics. Schmitt clearly feels sympathy for the anarchists, the syndicalists and the fascists, because they too see the world in either/or terms, even if he disagrees with them on substantive social issues. His real intellectual and political enemies are twofold: liberalism and a view of social organization as consisting in nothing more than practical matters of organizational-technical management. Like Max Weber he fears a world in which formal end-rational calculation comes to dominate social action. The result is that Schmitt's own position, for all its critical power, is curiously circumscribed: it insists upon the state of exception and yet seeks to stabilize it, and if possible to end it by positive political action. The humdrum affairs of management and bargaining between groups in a stabilized political condition are of no interest to Schmitt. Equally he resists the relentless nihilistic crusade of anarchism or fascism – he wishes to preserve a definite social order. To do so he relies on a dictator and on special state measures. He offers an essentially conservative counter-action in the absence of an adequate basis for political stability. But such dictators are suspended in a socio-political vacuum – like von Schleicher they must govern with nothing behind them.

Schmitt's relentless attack upon 'discussion' must surely make most modern radicals and democrats extremely hostile to his views. Schmitt is a relentless enemy of the Enlightenment. Habermas's 'ideal speech situation' in which we communicate without distortion to discover a common 'emancipatory interest' would appear to Schmitt as a philo-sophical re-statement of Francois Guizot's view that in representative government 'through discussion the powers-that-be are obliged to seek truth in common' (cited by Schmitt, *The Crisis of Parliamentary Democracy* (1985), p. 97, n. 5). Enemies cannot talk and we can never reach a world in which the friend–enemy distinction is abolished. Schmitt is probably right, liberalism does tend to ignore the exception and the more relentless forms of political struggle. But Schmitt's reasoning is left with the state of exception and nothing else. In a 'total state' with a relatively stabilized balance of political forces, Schmitt's doctrine has nothing much to teach us. There is something of a contradiction between his concepts of the political and the total state: the total state by making everything political infects the sphere of politics with the complex necessities of economic management and social organization. Schmitt can only see the total state as a destruction of liberalism, the end of the division between the state and civil society. But such a state reduces the scope of the either/or by vastly broadening the agenda of public business. Increasingly the 'state' is not the 'sovereign' body of political struggle, a decisive centre acting exceptionally, but a vast complex of ill-coordinated public-service agencies.

In such a complex public-service state, regulation and arbitration become essential and hence the need for a jurisprudence which pays regard to the character of the state as a public-service agency concerned with practical problems of social organization. Such problems are difficult to treat as matters of 'exacting moral decision', although that is what the contemporary New Right in fact try to do. They are matters of investigation, of balancing advantages, of paying due regard to outcomes – matters which in short require 'discussion'. This discussion will never be a seeking of truth in common; it is an approach to solving problems where there can seldom be 'truth'. Rather it is a mixture of analysis and evaluation concerned with existing states of affairs. Such a 'discussion' will recognize interests and seek to accommodate them – not to find 'the truth' or a 'morally exacting' solution.

In fact Schmitt's view of 'discussion' supposes a high-bourgeois polity of a type which has never existed. It treats parliament as a kind of collective reasoning agency. Schmitt's acceptance at face value of the liberal-democratic rationale for parliament is, however, neither naive nor just polemical. Schmitt insists that institutions require a principle or rationale that will command support. They cannot thrive simply because there is claimed to be no alternative to them. The question 'what else?' is hardly a rallying call. Like Weber in regard to the pre-1914 *Reichstag*, Schmitt held the Weimer Republic's assembly in some contempt. Both Weber and Schmitt judged parliamentarism in terms of liberal-democratic rhetoric and both found the practice wanting and Schmitt found the rationale wanting too. Weber wanted to marry parliamentarism and effective plebiscitary democracy, to make the parliamentary chamber an effective training ground for leaders. Such a function presupposes a chamber in which debate and genuine autonomy for its members still have a place.

In terms of modern pluralist political theory, parliament has ceased to play that crucial role. Schmitt and Weber could both be taken to task for seeing in the behaviour and nature of parties the failure of parliamentary institutions, whereas it is argued by modern pluralists that parliaments only function as a certain focus of the party system and they can never work better than that system does. Effective parliaments presuppose leading parties which can compromise because they operate within a consensus and which are strong enough to marginalize non-consensus parties. Schmitt certainly recognized that such a party system did not exist in Germany. Where such a system does exist then parliaments can be one effective instrument among others in party governments' political management, and a limited forum for trading between consensus parties' interests. Such parliaments are very different from Schmitt's view of parliamentarism as based on the principle of discussion but they also work very differently from the way representative government is supposed to in classic liberal-democratic theory.

In the Weimar Republic the state of exception was close to being the norm, and therefore the constitutional status and political function of the exceptional powers of the President were a serious matter of political debate. Schmitt used these practical debates to make general and challenging points about the nature of sovereignty and law. In most of the post-1945 Western democracies the state of exception in the form Schmitt knew it has become a marginal political problem. Political stability has permitted complacency in political theory, and, indeed, has required it as one of its conditions. But stably functioning party systems exist for reasons that have little to do with constitutional doctrine, and no amount of formally liberal measures can compensate for the decline of such a system. Nowhere in the West, despite growing strains and a less consensual political climate than in the 1950s, have parties reached the stage of antagonistic competition characteristic of Weimar with the exception of the period 1925–8. But parliamentary democracy has ceased to function as classic liberal-democratic theory supposes it to do. No one expects it to provide the forum for 'discussion' which Schmitt derided. But parliamentary institutions have ceased to superintend effectively the workings of modern big government. The 'total state' may have marginalized Schmitt's politics of 'morally exacting' decision but it has also marginalized existing methods of democratic supervision and control to a degree little recognized. Parliament has become a tool of party government, but even more so of big government in general – it has come to serve as a means of giving legitimacy and legality to the actions of the ramified mass of state agencies. Neither classic liberal-democratic theories not pluralist views of polyarchical competition in a stable party system can provide, without supplementation, an account of the organizational forms necessary for more effective democratic accountability.

Schmitt cannot do so either but his views on the nature of sovereignty are a valuable way of identifying certain contemporary problems of democratic control. Because Schmitt is no democrat he recognizes and insists upon things democrats often wish to forget. The modern state may restrict the scope for Schmitt's politics of either/or, imposing a mass of functions in which such 'political' thinking would be reactionary and counter-productive, but it remains a political association in Schmitt's sense. By and large, governmental agencies concerned with matters of social and economic organization operate through managerial imperatives and are subject to at least some minimal legal regulation and political control. But they do not exhaust the state. Schmitt is valuable because he stresses that all legal orders have an 'outside' and that definite agencies within the state have the capacity (if not the formal constitutional right) to act extra-legally. The consequences of modern states acting in this way are far greater than in Schmitt's day, the Nazis notwithstanding, because the organizational capacities and military power of the modern state are so much greater. The entire apparatus of nuclear security has escaped democratic political control in that the technology involved telescopes the time involved in operational decision-making so radically and restricts it to such a small circle of persons that it does become a simple matter of 'morally exacting' decision. In that sense, we do have a very clear 'sovereign' and a perpetual prospect of the state of exception. Friend–enemy relations have not disappeared, even if they are frozen by the consequences of pursuing them to the full between the Superpowers. Further, the effect of this condition on the rest of the polity is considerable. The nuclear security apparatus reserves itself to considerable powers of control over economic resources, special police measures, etc., and has a capacity for secret policy-making whose limits are difficult to determine. If we take Schmitt's claim that 'sovereign is he who decides on the exception' seriously, then most of our formal constitutional doctrines are junk.

'PLURALISM'

Schmitt was well informed about contemporary trends in political theory and jurisprudence, and knew of the work of Duguit and the English pluralists.[3] Of Duguit, Schmitt remarked:

> some have somewhat hastily proclaimed the death and end of the state . . . this emerged as a doctrine of the French syndicalists after 1906 and 1907. Duguit is in this context the best known political theorist. Ever since 1901 he has tried to refute the conception of sovereignty and the conception of the personality of the state with some accurate arguments against an uncritical metaphysics of the state, which are, after all, only remnants from the world of princely absolutism but in essence miss the actual political meaning of the concept of sovereignty. (*Concept of the Political*, p. 40)

Schmitt knew a serious adversary when he saw one. Duguit was not an anti-statist labour syndicalist but a supporter of administrative syndicalism, not anti-state but in favour of a modern concept of the state as a social organization. Schmitt sidesteps Duguit's analysis by relegating his challenge to the theory of sovereignty to the status of a critique of the obsolete political theology of the state rather than its real essence in the political. Duguit's views, in fact, represent a more adequate account of a major aspect of the 'total state' than Schmitt's own; its character as a collection of public-service agencies posing concrete problems of social and industrial organization. Duguit also poses a far harder challenge to Schmitt than the English pluralists. He does not share their liberal anti-statist assumptions nor is he tied, as Cole was, to radical projects for the total reconstruction of society. English pluralism is also in an important sense derivative of and heavily dependent upon continental theory: in the case of Figgis on a reading of Otto von Gierke and, in the case of Laski, on Duguit himself and Maurice Hauriou.

Duguit was a colleague of Durkheim's at Bordeaux and was greatly influenced by him.[4] Durkheim is worth considering as a preface to Duguit's views because, although he subscribed to the values of liberal individualism and representative government, he was as tough-minded and ruthless in respect of problems of the social order as Schmitt himself. Schmitt emphasizes political struggle; Durkheim recognizes it fully and seeks to subject it to social control. Durkheim's lectures on civic morals are a neglected work of political theory and one well worth considering as a foil to Schmitt.

Durkheim recognizes that the values of individualism and liberalism depend on definite organized collectives and hence upon patriotism and a measure of social discipline. Individualism is not a natural phenomenon as classical liberalism supposes but a social creation, 'morals are a product of the society . . . and they have force only so far as the society is organised' (*Professional Ethics*, p. 74). Like Schmitt, Durkheim rejects extreme anti-statist individualism, which can see only humanity and not definite nation states. He does so because the effect of those doctrines is 'to disparage the existing moral law' (ibid.), and not because they ignore the nature of friend–enemy groupings. 'The state is the highest form of organised society that exists' (ibid.) and, therefore, must be the focus of all concern with the existing social order. Durkheim perceives modern societies to be janus-faced. On the one hand, their liberal economic and social systems which we based on an extensive division of labour create a cult of the individual – this individualism Durkheim contends to be necessary. On the other hand, such societies take the form of nation states and demand from their members all the patriotic duties of the simpler collectivities of old, subjecting the individual to a discipline whose goal is the collectivity. Durkheim recognizes war as a condition which threatens in these conditions of social organization through nation states, although he is enough of an Enlightenment liberal to regard it as a hangover from the past. He correctly perceives in war, in political struggle between states, the basis of the state's power over the individual: 'War, of course, leads to a disregard of individual rights. It demands severe discipline and this discipline in turn presupposes a strongly entrenched authority. It is from this source there comes the sovereign power over individuals that is so often lodged in the state' (*Professional Ethics*, p. 53). Durkheim recognizes as clearly as Schmitt that a central aspect of political authority arises out of friend–enemy relations but, unlike Schmitt, he does not welcome this fact. He responds as any good nineteenth-century liberal would: the less often wars occur, 'the more possible and imperative it becomes to disarm the state. War has not yet entirely gone out and there are still threats of international rivalry: so the State . . . still has to preserve a measure of its former prerogatives. But here, in war, we have only something of an anomalous survival, and gradually the last traces of it are bound to be wiped out' (*Professional Ethics*, p. 53).

One can tell that this was written before 1914 – Durkheim is sure that the possibility of war between the Great Powers is no more than a barbarous survival. What is surprising is that Schmitt can be, if not sanguine, then at least matter-of-fact about war *after 1918*. He was quite right to denounce the liberal illusions of the 1920s, the era of Locarno and the League of Nations. But he seems relatively indifferent to the dangers of and the price paid for the 'morally exacting decision'. Durkheim – and Schmitt – are both right; until war and friend–enemy relations can be dramatically reduced or contained then the state will retain all its draconian prerogatives. In the modern world, the desire to forgo political struggle in Schmitt's sense, to base social affairs on 'discussion' not friend–enemy relations, is a rational one, although we can make no providentialist assumptions that it will become a dominant and successful one. Until it does, Schmitt's analysis of 'sovereignty' as the power to decide on the exception will stand and will make a mockery of all liberal and democratic conceptions of the state.

The alternative, however, cannot be a depoliticized utopia of concord and amity. To check social and national conflicts from 'going political', in Schmitt's sense, libertarian individualism and utopian socialism offer no effective answers because both in their different ways presuppose a natural harmony of interests. Durkheim, on the contrary, sees the need for social control and moral discipline. Durkheim approaches the problems of democracy and 'discussion' from an entirely different angle from either classical parliamentary liberalism or from Schmitt.

Durkheim argues that the state has become a complex of public service functions; a directing 'social-brain' that organizes and regulates the complex affairs of a differentiated society characterized by an extensive division of labour. Durkheim argues 'the state is nothing if it is not an organ distinct from the rest of society (*Professional Ethics*, p. 82). If it were not, then it could not perform its organizing and regulatory functions. In all societies, except the most simple, the actual business of government is always carried out by an organized minority, and in this respect there is actually little difference between governmental forms. What is crucial for democracy is not the exact method by which that minority of persons are selected but how the governmental organs communicate with the rest of society. Viewed in this manner as the 'organ of social thought' (*Professional Ethics*, p. 79) and as an agency with a specific task to do, one of regulation and coordination, then authoritarian views of the state as a relation between the sovereign as a person and individual subjects are inapposite and obsolete. What we may call in Foucault's terms the 'juridico-discursive' concept of power cannot cope with the major modern role of the state – the question at issue is a relation of communication and control, not of social distance and authoritative power of command. Durkheim stresses how weak were the absolute monarchies which proclaimed, in their political ideology, this juridico-discursive view of power:

> They were all-powerful against the individual and this is what the term 'absolute' means as applied to them. But against the social condition itself, against the structure of society, they are relatively powerless. Louis XIV, clearly, was able to issue his *Lettres de cachet* against anyone he wished, but he had no power to modify the existing laws and usages, the established customs or excepted beliefs. (*Professional Ethics*, p. 87)

Durkheim claims that if we compare the small scope of seventeenth-century government deliberation, concerned at best with war, police and justice, with the ramified complexities of modern government business, we can see why the systematic communication between states and society has become essential.

Durkheim's view of democracy is neither a liberal nor a populist one. Democracy consists for Durkheim not in specific representative mechanisms but in the degree and quality of the communication between government and society. Democracy is necessary because, in a complex public-service state, governmental practices must be effectual and, therefore, based on empirically sound information about their reception by society. Durkheim says: 'Reflection alone makes possible the discovery of new and effectual practices, for it is only by reflection that the future can be anticipated. This is why deliberative assemblies are becoming ever more widely accepted as an institution' (*Professional Ethics*, p. 90). The complexity of modern social organization and the ramified tasks of government in regulating it both enforces the need for reflection in politics and restricts the scope of the 'morally exacting decision' and its basis in prejudice or tradition. Democracy is thus a process of two-way communication between state and society based upon empirical and rational considerations of efficacy: 'The more that deliberation, reflection and a critical spirit play a considerable part in the course of public affairs, the more democratic the nation' (*Professional Ethics*, p. 89). Not the extent of the franchise but the nature of the political process determines how democratic a nation is.

What is the difference between Durkheim and Guizot? Is not Durkheim just another liberal 'seeker after truth'? Well, not exactly. Firstly, parliament and government conceived as the higher executive organs have only a secondary part in this scheme. Far from being 'sovereign', as they would be in doctrines that seek to give expressoin to the people's will, they are merely part of a complex process of communication and administration. At best the National Assembly and the Council of Ministers coordinate ideas and sentiments; they stand at the apex of a pyramid of continuously acting specialist agencies. Secondly, Durkheim seeks to supplement parliamentary democracy with other forms of representation. In Schmitt's concept of democracy, homogeneity is central, the 'people' become an exclusive body defined against others. For Durkheim the people as such is far from homogeneous. Indeed, Durkheim is concerned that the division of labour has so fragmented society that few of its members are regulated in their everyday lives by an effective moral order related to work. Durkheim's answer to this pathology of the division of labour is a modernized guild system; a supplement to the representation of individual voters in the form of the representation of corporate occupational groups. Democracy, in Durkheim's theory, is anything but a populist and plebiscitarian power.

Durkheim's view of corporatist representation and regulation of economic groupings has often been criticized by radical sociologists and socialists as an absurd attempt to mediate between the irreconcilable powers of capital and labour. Viewed as part of his doctrine of democracy it makes some sense; if the state is the organ of social thought, and therefore of coordination and control, then it depends on close and continuous contact with social affairs. The idea of a minimally regulated 'private sphere', which in fact absorbs the mass of the population for a large part of the day and upon which their livelihood depends, is contrary to Durkheim's view of social coordination. How can social control be effective if people's working lives are not morally regulated to some common social end and according to collective standards? How can individuals be integrated into the collective life if they are supposed to be governed by non-moral 'interests' of a purely personal character? How can it be acceptable if workers and capitalists alike approach industrial problems in terms of narrow considerations of personal pecuniary advantage and without regard for the good of the industrial service performed for society? If workers can be treated as on a par with machines, as mere means to an end, then they will regard their place of labour and their tasks with a similar instrumentality.

Durkheim's diagnosis of the moral malaise of modern industry extends not merely to capitalism but also to its anticipated solution in socialism. He rejects both the authoritarian scientism of Saint Simon and the Marxist and syndicalist rhetoric of 'class struggle' (Durkheim, *Socialism and Saint-Simon* (1962)). The conventional doctrines of socialism do not offer the prospect of an economic system subject to effective moral regulation. Durkheim proposes a solution which involves both regulation of individual members' acts by their professional association, and economic coordination through the representation of associations in the state. The primary purpose of the system of guilds is not 'economic', unlike much modern thinking about corporate bargaining (which merely turns the anomic private 'interests' of individuals into organized collectivities), but of subjecting economic life to moral rules concerned with social order, the welfare of society as a whole, and the policing conduct of individuals such that they treat one another as ends rather than means. Durkheim's corporatism may be a little hazy about institutional mechanisms and economic effects but it is neither anti-worker nor authoritarian. The state is not the primary partner in the relationship with the new industrial guilds nor is it the 'sovereign state' of classical political theory, but a public-service state. Durkheim's version of corporatism has nothing in common with the demagogic anti-democratic ideas of Mussolini; it implies neither a regulation of labour on behalf of the capitalist owners of the means of production nor an authoritarian power of direction of industry by the state.

Durkheim's view of the state as a public-service agency with a continuous and multiform relation to society implies a public-law doctrine very different from traditional doctrines based on sovereignty. It is this that Duguit's jurisprudence offers. For Duguit the legal regulation of the state's agencies and their relation to society must take account of the objective requirements of social organization. The state has certain functions to perform and statutes and rules simply establish the framework for such a service to meet a need. Legislation is not, therefore, privileged because it is issued by a 'sovereign' body, rather it must first of all make operational and administrative sense. In consequence, Duguit argues, the working of laws is increasingly subject to processes of judicial review directly concerned with the effect of these laws as public policy. Likewise, rule-making and regulation-setting powers develop in agencies other than the legislature. Public officials are not the privileged servants of a sovereign power and above public regulation because they are the agents of an authoritarian power of command. They are public officials whose conduct may be regulated by the courts and their acts assessed in terms of whether they correspond to their obligations in providing a service. Likewise, there can be no simple separation of the public and the private sphere; contracts and obligations must be considered in terms of the need to perform a service.

Duguit recognizes an industrial and social-service state undreamt of in the classic liberal-democratic theories. He perceives an army of public servants and a whole array of public-service agencies whose continuous functioning cannot be adequately regulated by the Council of Ministers or the legislative assembly. He starts from the reality of delegated authority and delegated rule-making powers, insisting on the superficiality of the view of the state as being directed by a single legislative or executive 'will'. He starts with the issue of a complex state system, which requires a new institutional order and a new jurisprudence. Duguit is far too sanguine in supposing that the 'technical' needs of running a service will provide an impartial and empirical basis for the legal superintendence of administrative acts. He is also naive in imagining that French administrative law, the doctrine of *ultra-vires* as a means of regulating state agencies' and state servants' actions, and the Council of State could serve as adequate means to control the new 'total state'.

Duguit supports administrative decentralization: the recognition of powers of rule-making and decision at the appropriate level, with a definite degree of autonomy for the organs of service in question and their personnel. The industrial service state makes such administrative decentralization necessary if tasks are to be effectively administered and if the load of control is to be reduced to manageable levels in the higher executive and legislative organs. The implication, as Durkheim pointed out, is that the legislative assembly and the council of ministers are not 'sovereign', and cannot substitute themselves for lesser authorities or ignore their advice. Such a system requires a jurisprudence objective enough to mediate between public service agencies as to their powers, and also to mediate between them and citizens as to their obligations in performing a service.

Like Schmitt, Duguit attacks the political theory of the liberal-parliamentary era. He treats the classic doctrine of sovereignty as a 'myth' contrary to fact. He claims: 'With some rare exceptions there was no class or party in the nineteenth century which did not accept national sovereignty as a religious dogma' (*Law in the Modern State* (1921), p. 15). The modern doctrine of national sovereignty transfers the king's sovereign powers to the 'nation'. But the 'nation' is seldom more then a polite fiction for the more-or-less heterogeneous population of a state. The will of the 'nation' is always expressed through its representatives. National sovereignty is a simple transfer of the claim of proprietal power on the part of the king to dispose over his kingdom and to command its subjects. Duguit shows how the French Revolution simply appropriated the *these royale* and attributed its claim to unlimited powers of law-making and command to the people's representatives. Sovereignty as the collective will is treated as the absolute power of an uncommanded commander; the state is conceived as a person. To this the Revolution added the contradictory notion of the inalienable rights of the individual. This leads to a subjectivist jurisprudence in which two subjects and two wills stand in tension: the sovereign subject commands; its commands are legitimate because they are the will of the people refracted through the state; the individual obeys as a loyal citizen – provided, that is, there is no infringement of his or her inalienable rights implied in the command. The power to command is thus trebly problematic:

1 First, it treats the state as a person, with a single will, rather than a number of agencies and persons with different tasks and means of decision;
2 Second, it supposes that the state expresses a coherent 'will of the people', as if there were such an entity;
3 Third, it supposes that the sovereign power and the inalienable rights of the individual can be made compatible.

The theological derivation of these ideas is self-evident in that they generate the need for the political equivalent of a theodicy; a demonstration that a boundless sovereign power can respect individual rights and observe the rule of law. Rousseau's *Social Contract* offered just such a political theodicy. It reconciled the boundless sovereignty of the general will with the freedom of the individual. But, like all such efforts to explain the inexplicable, it cannot withstand the slightest threat from scepticism. Once we ask how is it that God is good, we are well on the way to denying that He exists at all.

Yet, if Rousseau's conjuring trick is widely seen as such, the absurd structure first erected in 1791 resists all scepticism. Indeed, modern political argument admits of less room for scepticism than was available at the beginning of this century. Duguit was far from naive, he did not imagine the state was nothing more than a collection of sanitary inspectors and public tram-lines. The state involves force and coercive power, but it is a complexly organized force and not the pure force of the sovereign will. But that sovereign will and the inalienable rights of the individual remain central elements in modern liberal-democratic political doctrine and practice. Contemporary liberal ideologues dream of a 'private sphere' and guaranteed individual rights – from the right to the left of liberalism, from von Hayek to Dworkin. Governments like Mrs Thatcher's use the doctrine of the 'sovereignty' of Parliament as a means to rationalize their attempt to manage and superintend the complex industrial and public-service state of the contemporary United Kingdom. That the results of trying to undo administrative decentralization, and that largely through the public cashbox, have led to disorder and maladministration is self-evident. Other examples in the Western world are less extreme, but the baleful consequences of the doctrine of 'sovereignty' and its supposed basis in the 'will of the people' should be self-evident. Modern political discourse is simultaneously addicted to sovereignty and human rights. We need something more appropriate to the late twentieth-century to replace this eighteenth-century rhetoric; a political doctrine sufficiently complex to cope with the modern public-service state and also with the 'total state' in which the private sphere is no sacred domain, but largely a matter of administrative and policy convenience.

It would be silly to imagine either Durkheim or Duguit would provide an adequate political doctrine. They are limited and old-fashioned because in the intervening decades there has been almost no thought on these issues, no theoretical development, and little criticism. Likewise, we have no theorizing adequate to cope with Schmitt's proposition, 'sovereign is he who decides on the exception', and with its practical application in the modern nuclear-state security apparatus. Most theorizing on such issues merely notes how 'undemocratic' or 'out of control' such agencies and technologies are, or proposes some com-munitarian pre-industrial Luddism as the answer. Schmitt points to the problem that, until we contain 'the political', we shall have a 'sovereign' power quite different from that fantasized as the 'people's will'. But he also demonstrates that we cannot wish the political away by providen-tialist assumptions about a world without conflict. We need to pose the problem of a framework of moral order and social control sufficient to contain conflicts within and between nation states. A conception of such a framework which does not repeat the authoritarian illusions of a sovereign power which imposes peace, and yet which has the capacity to compel discussion and deliberation, is a very tall order. It implies constraint, without making that constraint issue from the commands of superior or sovereign subjects. Durkheim posed the problem even if he could not solve it. Schmitt showed why a solution was necessary in spite of himself.

8

Carl Schmitt: decisionism and political romanticism

If Carl Schmitt had quietly left Germany in January 1933 he would now be remembered internationally as that country's leading legal and political theorist of the twentieth century. Schmitt did not catch the train, nor did he join that legion of German conservatives who submitted to Nazism in silence, only to re-emerge as leading figures in the Federal Republic. A leading conservative critic of the Nazis, an advocate of presidential rule by emergency decree to exclude them from political power, Schmitt went over to them in an astounding and unprincipled *volte face* in 1933. He remained a Nazi, increasingly disregarded and dishonoured by the Party, until 1945. For the next four decades Schmitt was a non-person in the Anglo-Saxon intellectual world and a bitterly controversial figure in the Federal Republic.

Why not leave it that way? Surely it is best for us non-Germans to leave in obscurity a man who actively and cynically collaborated with Nazism? Even if this were desirable, it is no longer possible. Schmitt's reputation as a political thinker has been growing steadily, in Italy, and now in the Anglo-Saxon world. Schmitt's *The Concept of the Political* was translated in 1976, three translations in the series 'Studies in Contemporary German Social Thought', edited by Thomas McCarthy, have followed, *Political Theology* and *The Crisis of Parliamentary Democracy* in 1985 and *Political Romanticism* in 1986. Joseph Bendersky's major biography was published in 1983. Attention to Schmitt's work is by no means part of some neo-conservative revival; on the contrary, his main reception outside Germany is by the left.

Why do sections of the left take Carl Schmitt seriously? On the face of it, Schmitt's adoption by the left seems rather odd. Even before 1933, Schmitt was a determined critic of parliamentary liberalism, of liberal-positivist theories of the *Rechtsstaat* and of the values of the Enlightenment. Schmitt was not a radical, not even a fascist radical, but a firm defender of the constitution as a bulwark of the existing social order. To see why Schmitt is taken seriously and why he is also bitterly controversial one has only to look at the current situation in radical political theorizing. In September 1986, Jürgen Habermas published a long article on Schmitt in *The Times Literary Supplement*. His response to the publication of Schmitt in English is symptomatic of the controversy on the left surrounding this figure of the right. Habermas tried at one and the same time to be fair, to explain Schmitt to a non-German audience, and also to isolate him in a specifically German context, to marginalize him for Anglo-Saxon readers.

Habermas's increasing dominance of the democratic left in modern political theory is a victory for both the virtues and the illusions of the Enlightenment. Habermas's enterprise is popular because it offers a substitute for the increasingly discredited orthodox Marxist conception of politics and a challenge to the relativist and opportunist 'postmodernist' conception of politics increasingly influential among sections of the Western intelligentsia. Habermas's critical theory is radical in challenging the dominance of technocratic administration and mass manipulation, and yet offers as its basis for criticism an alternative order founded on rational and consensual norms. Habermas's criticism attempts to go beyond existing institutions but not to destroy democracy and liberal values.

Schmitt was a critic of parliamentary liberalism precisely because he did not think that the state and politics could be exclusively defined in terms of law. Liberalism's conception of a *Rechtsstaat* supposes a stable and exhaustive normative order. Parliamentary politics is discussion about policy within the consensus formed by that order and that discussion leads on to laws and lawful administration. Schmitt denies that politics can be bound by norms. As he explains in *The Concept of the Political* the essence of politics is struggle, friend–enemy relations. In *Political Theology* he argues that it is the state of exception which defines the norm, and not the other way round. It is political authority, power arising from struggle, that determines when things can be normal, when settled regimes of law are possible. Schmitt insists that *all* legal orders have an outside. Politics and the state are not in fact bound by law, and political necessity knows no law; in the last instance it seeks political order by means that are without law. To a man who witnessed the 1918 Munich uprising, who lived in a world where the *Freikorps* and the *SA* walked the streets, these were factual statements about politics and not right-wing fancies. If one were to spend but little time looking at the preparations made in this country for a wartime state of exception to apply if nuclear weapons were ever used or if there were a massive nuclear accident one might feel a little more like Schmitt. In a legal-positivist sense these exceptional measures are lawful, but they know no norm intelligible to liberalism. Sovereign indeed is he who decides on the exception.

Schmitt insisted that we must take account of the essence of the political as struggle and the determination of legal normality by its opposite, its out-law, the exception. Yet, in spite of this lesson, he did not want antagonistic political struggle and the exception to become the rule. On the contrary, his legal thought is obsessed with the containment and suppression of states of exception. Schmitt saw clearly the blindness of *Rechtsstaatlich* liberalism in the face of these facts; as doctrine it had simply no room to accommodate them.

Habermas, like many other critics, regards Schmitt's conception of the 'essence' of the political as friend–enemy relations as simplistic, abstract and one-sided, in no sense a fully social-scientific analytical concept of political power. Schmitt was not seeking a comprehensive concept of political power, but the essential feature that makes politics different from other spheres like economics or religion which may involve administration, authority and goal-oriented cooperation. That feature is struggle, and struggle means the reciprocal action of parties opposed to one another. Schmitt's concept is no more inadequate than is Clausewitz's concept of the essence of war as the combat, at its simplest two wrestlers fighting. Schmitt, like Clausewitz in the military sphere, and like Machiavelli in the matter of statecraft, sees politics as dominated by reciprocal action.[1] In such a world decisions, not norms, are dominant. At the extreme, no norm unites friend and enemy, but imposed on each of them is the need for decision. Such conflicts are inclusive and one must choose. It is the conflict which sets the terms of choice, not a norm. Political struggle imposes the morally exacting decision, the either/or. Morality is defined by choice, good or evil by the terms offered. There is no rule above the choice, and discussion cannot resolve the opposing forces.

Schmitt's 'decisionistic' view of politics, morality and law certainly cannot stand on its own, but it is a vital corrective to a view of politics bound by norms and concerned with pre-political morally defined goals. Kant, in *On Perpetual Peace* (1795), tried to show the superiority of the normatively directed 'moral politician', who followed an ethically sound maximum of conduct consistently.[2] The pragmatic politician, in contrast, will use any means, and faces in consequence a heteronomy of direction; expediency dictates the course of action. The result is inconstancy and, therefore, ultimately inefficacy. Kant's criticism is sound only on certain definite conditions; it supposes a world where all action is legal and peaceful, and where one is free to set out and exclusively pursue one's ends. But that is not politics as Schmitt conceives it. Kant's general conception of political action is rationalistic, concerned only with an actor, ends and means. It simply ignores the necessities imposed by reciprocal action and struggle between actors, viewing politics ethically and judicially. Such a view is necessary, indeed, salutory, but it is no substitute for a view like Schmitt's.

Reciprocal action means that one can be driven by the opponent's moves, if one does not anticipate the competition and drive it instead. One may propose a morality which resists this logic of competition, one should pursue ethically sound maxims of conduct regardless of the concrete results. That may be ethically magnificent but it is not politics. Only if reciprocal action and struggle can be eliminated can norms unreservedly prevail over decisions. Only if politics can be replaced by other spheres of action like administration or religion can rationality or morality prevail over political choice. Schmitt envisages no end to politics. The matter of politics, *what* friend–enemy relations are about, is an open question. Whenever there is a plurality of actors, differing constructions by those actors of their interests, and the possibility of conflict between them, then *any* activity can go political. A world in which politics was eliminated would be one in which there was only one answer for everybody. It supposes a rational norm of scientific means–ends calculation that converts all action into administration or a normative order with exhaustive repertoires of prescribed conduct, such as one finds in monastic orders. Schmitt denies the post-political world of Marxism's classless utopia in which 'the domination of man by man is replaced by the administration of things.' He also denies the post-political world of a liberal utopia in which procedural norms reduce politics to no more than debate or discussion.

Schmitt's decisionism is neither self-consciously irrationalist nor nihilistic. It is not a subjectification of politics. Like Machiavelli, Schmitt has suffered from pointing to the conditions of politics, explaining that they are non-optional for political actors and demonstrating how you play to win. Like Machiavelli he believes in an economy of violence and like him he subscribes to a political morality quite different from that of Sunday schools or civics classes.[3] The moralistic and rationalistic tirades against both are rather similar: believers in rational and binding norms hate the idea of unavoidable and primitive moral choices in politics. Schmitt is certainly an ethical relativist; choices are contextual. Schmitt believes morality is made by choosing and in conditions so primitive that reflection is no great help. Schmitt is certainly an existentialist, in the sense that norms are governed by choices not the other way around.

Schmitt does not romanticize choice, despite Habermas's claim that he aestheticizes the political actor. On the contrary, Schmitt's view is absolutely unromantic: to choose is to decide, to decide is to act, to act is to face an opponent, and because one faces an opponent the consequences of one's actions are unavoidable. The consequences of the political romantic's aestheticizing posture are always avoidable because the romantic is careful not to act. The romantic strikes political poses in a politically safe world of stabilized bourgeois norms. Outside that world one pays the price for one's actions. The romantic can be caught posturing, having foolishly strayed into the political scene. Political romantics like Drieu La Rochelle made exactly this mistake when they flirted with fascism. Schmitt did not flirt with fascism; he chose Hitler. He paid for it, in part, with forty years of silence, but not in full measure.

One can see why Habermas should wish to reject Schmitt's ideas. Habermas's critical standpoint depends on a condition of rational consensus, of discussion in a context of norms that permit us to reach a common answer. This process is based on the assumptions that undistorted rational communication is possible and that we all share a common objective emancipatory interest. Schmitt's decisionism says this is moonshine. Less immediately apparent is why Habermas's relation to Schmitt is so uneasy. A recent article by Ellen Kennedy in *Telos* aroused heated controversy because she considered Schmitt's relation to members of the Frankfurt School (Kennedy, 'Carl Schmitt and the Frankfurt School', *Telos* (1987)). In fact Habermas's conception of an ideal democracy implies homogeneity, a radical identity of interests that makes rational debate possible. Schmitt always insisted that homogeneity is a pre-condition for democracy, that it implies an identity of interests for its decision-making procedures to be tolerable. Only by making extreme assumptions can Habermas square universal participation and a democratically decidable will of the people; Habermas requires a rational consensus to square an acceptable normative order with a democratic power of decision.

Habermas says that Schmitt's really problematic move is the separation of democracy and liberalism. But problematic for whom? Habermas can only unite them at the price of a fantastic superstructure of rationalistic social theory. Outside of Habermas's fairy tale, liberalism and democracy are, indeed, in tension. The left political theorists who adopt Schmitt do so because of the power of his criticism of representative democracy. Schmitt argued that the liberal-parliamentary political order rested on a series of depoliticizations in which religion, economic affairs and so on were made matters of the private action of individuals in civil society. Parliament could then serve as the 'dis-interested' forum of the bourgeois political order, where policy limited in content could be debated by bourgeois notables whose livelihoods and beliefs were secure in civil society. But these depoliticizations break down with the development of a 'total state' charged with social regulation and economic management. Parliament becomes the forum of the antagonistic interests in society and discussion is replaced by bargaining and the construction of coalitions of representatives' votes to form majorities. Representative democracy in a total state shows the dangers of democratic procedures without homogeneity. A mere 51 per cent (in our case 42 per cent) of the vote provides victors with the legal and state power to determine how others shall live. In a total state the losers can no longer take refuge in the depoliticized spheres of life. Such a system unites the *Rechtsstaatlich* formal power of the rule of law with state power over all areas of life legitimated by a plebiscite.

The relic of the liberal order is the doctrine of the rule of law. Legality now legitimates the power of big government to write its own rules and to intervene where the ruling parties legitimated by the plebiscite will it to. The rule of law remains formally but has little substance, since there are fewer and fewer autonomous decisions regulated but not directed by law. Laws change their character from regulatory norms to administrative instruments. In a weak state with strongly antagonistic political parties, like Weimar, the façade of liberalism contributes to the collapse of the political order. We can see that Schmitt's analysis extends beyond Weimar to a strong state with a dominant, electorally legitimated ruling party. That is a stability Schmitt would favour, but nevertheless one in which democracy is the plebiscite which sanctions the rule of a fraction of society and the liberal legal order is a cloak for administrative action.

Franz Neumann, a leftist and a member of the Frankfurt School, developed Schmitt's ideas and used them in his concept of totalitarianism.[4] Schmitt's indication of the contradiction between liberalism and plebiscitary democracy in a total state shows how little restraint modern representative democracy offers to big government and mass administration. Schmitt was, moreover, not the only German-speaking critic to emphasize this contradiction. Mass democracy and the rule of interests broaden the agenda until everything is political. The liberal legal order is then at the mercy of the state in its attempts to appease mass demands. F. A. von Hayek, like Schmitt, perceived this effect of the antagonism of plebiscitary democracy and the liberal legal order.[5] In his case he self-consciously set out to plead for a state and society insulated against big government and demagogic mass-welfare politics. Hayek's work is an attempt to restore the depoliticizations crucial to the liberal order and restore the state to its normative and regulative role. Hayek's project is self-consciously conservative, it seeks to restore the conditions for a vanished liberal legal order. Schmitt's work, by contrast, is critical and because it was not tied to an explicit political programme, can be used to expose the contradictions of modern representative democracy without subscribing to Schmitt's own political values. It is a critique which de-mystifies without relying on a utopian end-state, an anti-politics.

Habermas is surprised that sections of the left should respond to the failure of Marxism as a political critique by using some of Schmitt's ideas. He claims that the left are 'filling the gap left by the non-existant Marxist theory of democracy with the Schmitt's fascist critique of democracy' ('Sovereignty and the Führerdemokratie', *Times Literary Supplement*, 26 September 1986, p. 1054). Far from being non-existant, Marxism's theory of democracy was of a popular participatory commune democracy in a society of great homogeneity and with only a single interest. Marxism's democracy testifies to the power of Schmitt's analysis. The closer the post-capitalist system comes to full realization, the more it becomes anti-political, without struggle or conflicting interests. Marxism's communist utopia is just as anti-political and socially homogeneous as Habermas's own political ideal which is to serve as the point of criticism of existing politics.

Schmitt's critique cannot be simply stigmatized by using the word 'fascist'; its critical power is by no means tied to a fascist politics. Schmitt is presented as the gravedigger of Weimar democracy, as if one constitutional lawyer, however eloquent, could bring down a system with any powers of survival or recuperation. Schmitt could equally be presented as a voice seeking to save the constitution at the expense of the parties. Schmitt catalogued the failure of Weimar and he was far from wrong about the causes of that failure. Modern democracies are not failing in the same way. On the contrary, they are succeeding all too well as devices for the legitimation and legalization of a state authority which is neither liberal nor democratic. It is a measure of Schmitt's perspicacity that his critique, shaped by Weimar's antagonistic pluralism, can be adapted to quite different conditions.

We can now turn from the context in which Schmitt's ideas have become important matter for debate to consider one of his most seminal works, which addresses contemporary problems although it is seventy years old. *Political Romanticism* is one of Schmitt's earliest works, first published in 1919. A book concerned with Friedrich Schlegel's and Adam Müller's political ideas, in the context of debates about the nature of nineteenth-century romanticism, might seem an odd choice for a contemporary series to translate when major works like *Legalität und Legitimität* remain untranslated. In fact *Political Romanticism* is a valuable work on two counts; one is that it clearly formulates Schmitt's decisionistic theory of ethics and political action, and the other is the concept of political romanticism itself. If anything political romanticism is a more real and problematic theoretical trend today than it was in the early years of the Weimar Republic. Romanticism is portrayed by Schmitt as a way out of the either/or, as an evasion of real political responsibility. The essence of political romanticism is political passivity coupled with an aestheticization of politics. A decision, left or right, whatever its legitimation, whether claiming to defend human rights or to preserve tradition, gives rise to political energy. Political energies lead to conflict and struggle.

Romanticism, on the contrary, aestheticizes political ideas and institutions. Politics is invested with emotion and it is the response of the subject to politics that becomes decisive. Political objects are aestheticized; they become sublime, and politics itself becomes a matter for subjective non-political emotional response. The romantic, bound by no decision, driven by no political energy, is thus free of the constraints of real politics. Free of engagement in struggle, the romantic is bound by none of the positions he or she adopts. The romantic avoids definite commitments by irony, by treating existing political forms as inadequate fulfilments of possibilities. Hence the political mobility of a romantic like Adam Müller between one political view and another. Hence also the presence of political romanticism on both the left and the right of the political spectrum.

For Schmitt, decisions are binding; they have moral force, precisely because they are choices in a conflict. One is bound within the either/or structure of real politics. The romantic is possible only on the basis of highly unromantic political and social facts. If the romantic subject makes its own experience the decisive judge of all phenomena, aestheticizing and subjectifying politics into the equivalent of a novel (*roman*), this is because of the security of a bourgeois order based on rules. Politically passive, the romantic is parasitic on an order in which political attitudes and poses lack consequences. One could be safely 'for' or 'against' the French Revolution in Germany; it was a matter of attitudinalizing in poems, newspaper articles and books in a safe and law-abiding world.

Schmitt calls romanticism a 'subjectified occasionalism'. He used the analogy of the occasionalistic metaphysics of Malebranche in which matter and spirit were reconciled. Cartesian dualism is avoided by a metaphysics in which material events and the soul are linked as alike occasions of God's will. The romantic regards all institutions, events, ideas and persons as an *occasio* for some response of the romantic. The romantic subject invests them with life; they become the starting point for a subjective investment. The romantic subject creates aesthetically and emotionally charged entities which resolve the antitheses and contradictions of real political life, 'third forces' which act like Malebranche's God. Politics is thus peopled with imaginary actors and agencies that turn politics into stories with desirable outcomes. Aestheticization substitutes for political struggle the outcomes desired by the subject and writes the romance in which they come true.

Political romanticism involves three elements: the subjectification of politics, aestheticizing as a substitute for political decision and occasionalism in which politics is resolved by imaginary forces. Political romanticism is not confined to the nineteenth century but can exist wherever 'a bourgeois world . . . isolates the individual in the domain of the intellectual, makes the individual its own point of reference, and imposes on it the entire burden that otherwise was hierarchically distributed among the different functions in a social order' (*Political Romanticism*, p. 20). Political romanticism is at once a function of that isolation – the individual defines politics subjectively – and an attempt to get out of it – the romantic individual uses politics in the occasionalistic mode to overcome his or her own isolation by imagining its resolution through a third force. Germany was saturated with such romanticism in the twenties and thirties – rightist intellectuals and youth movements aestheticizing and romanticizing the Volk, leftist intellectuals the proletariat. Walter Benjamin understood as clearly as Schmitt the dangers of an aestheticizing response to politics. In 'The Work of Art in the Age of Mechanical Reproduction', he cites Emilio Marinetti's appalling celebration of war as the ultimate outcome of an aestheticization of politics.

An aestheticized and romanticized politics is by no means always fascist in outlook. Benjamin is often cited as saying that the dominance of political action by aesthetic considerations is always fascist in effect. There are notable examples to sustain the point. *Triumph of the Will* is an aestheticization of the already politically romantic, the rally as an emotionally sublime work of art. But political romanticism is to be found on the left as well as the right and it seldom rises to Leni Riefenstahl's level. Usually far from being dangerous it is just histrionic and pathetic. The translator of Political Romanticism, Guy Oakes, in a valuable introduction cites as an example of the pathetic romanticization of politics Norman Mailer's *Armies of the Night*. The student movement of 1968 provided a veritable theatre of political romanticism.

Political romanticism is alive and well precisely because the isolated and subjectified intellectual thrives as never before. The 'death of the subject' does not mean the end of subjectivism. A great deal of 'postmodernist' political thinking and cultural criticism is nothing but the highest stage of political romanticism. A 'postmodernist' intelligentsia, that frivolously and half-comprehendingly follows Derrida, Foucault and Lacan, may set little store by the constitutive conscious subject, but actually they have little else left but a wilful, playful and anchorless subjectivity. Aestheticizing, playing with themes and devices in a subjectivist way, dominated by irony and the desire to create a certain mood, is inevitable if one believes there is no cultural work to be done. Subjectifying politics, making it a matter of *occasio*, but without a grand imaginary resolution, is inevitable if one believes that the meta-narratives of politics (often themselves products of political romanticism) have no mobilizing or legitimating power. As if politics came from 'meta-narratives' rather than from things sticking in one's throat. An intelligentsia safe enough in its Western cities and campuses, denied comforting myths about history and the working class, deprived of functions by mass culture and mass administration, has little left but to make political despair, relativism and the end of intellectual and moral order the occasion for its own political *tristesse*. Habermas clearly and rightly loathes such people. But Carl Schmitt provided a clear diagnosis of the 'postmodern' political romantic even as he wrote about Adam Müller. If Schmitt's reception is seen as a symptom of a loss of political energy and goals, as another symptom of the 'postmodern' condition, that would be a mistake. Schmitt is one of the best antidotes to the modern forms of political romanticism. One must be careful, however, in using Schmitt's work, not to forget or to excuse the decision made by the author.

9

Peace and political theory

Modern intellectuals are heirs to the Renaissance-humanist and Enlightenment view of war as a futile waste of human life and economic
resources. It is this view which explains the studied neglect of war in
modern liberal social and political theory. War is an abnormal political
condition and one destined to be historically transient with the march of
intellectual, moral and economic progress. The advent of nuclear
weapons has massively reinforced this view. Indeed, it has made it
appear wholly convincing for the first time. Hitherto, moralists could
defend the justice of war in certain circumstances, economists could
point to the beneficial effects for particular national economies of
having fought wars, and politicians and generals could demonstrate why
in certain circumstances war was a necessary and rational 'continuation
of policy by other means'. The realities of nuclear war abolish these
arguments. Intellectuals have had little trouble in demolishing arguments for deterrance as a stable condition, that is, as a viable armed
peace that prevents war by military means alone and without political
institutionalization.

What no one has been able to do is to analyse peace as a political
condition, to provide a political alternative to an unstable deterrance
which has lasted longer than we have a right to expect. I will be told I am
ignoring the vast outpouring of literature from the Peace Movement. I
can say with some certainty that I am not. That literature proves that
nuclear war is immoral, disastrous and too likely to happen to be
ignored. For comfort, the Peace Movement advocates 'disarmament' as
a primary political goal and CND advocates Britain disarming un-
ilaterally and unconditionally, as a moral lead to the rest of the nuclear
powers. I can find in British Peace-Movement writing no political
analysis of *how* to achieve nuclear disarmament among the Great
Powers, only pious invocations that it *should* happen and the belief that
it will happen if enough people commit themselves to it. This is no more

than the high-minded stock-in-trade of the 'liberal conscience' and it repeats a politics of moral earnestness, in other words, a non-politics, which has been with us since the nineteenth century.[1]

One solution, which is not new, is peddled across a wide spectrum of opinion, from the passionate plea against nuclear weapons we find in Jonathan Schell's *The Fate of the Earth* (1982) to the sober account of the development of military power in this millenium one finds in William McNeill's *The Pursuit of Power* (1983), and that is some form of world government with a monopoly of the means of making nuclear arms. McNeill puts this in the extreme form of an 'empire of the earth':

> To halt the arms race, political change appears to be necessary. A global sovereign power willing and able to enforce a monopoly of atomic weaponry could afford to disband research teams and dismantle all but a token number of warheads . . . an empire of the earth could be expected to limit violence by preventing other groups from arming themselves so elaborately as to endanger the sovereign's easy superiority. (McNeill, *Pursuit of Power*, p. 384)

How would this chilling 'empire', this Leviathan of Leviathans, accomplish this prevention? Either by pre-emptive nuclear strikes on research facilities or the threat of the same, or, by possessing an effective monopoly of conventional force such that it could, against opposition, enter and close any suspect research or production facility. Such a state could never be a democracy – McNeill is right to call it an 'empire' – and no confederal system could act with the ruthless singlemindedness necessary to ensure this monopoly of force.[2] A 'global sovereign power' with an effective monopoly of the means of violence would not limit itself to preventing war and would become a real 'empire of the earth'. Such a power might be preferable to a charred cinder turning silently in space, but not much. It is a fantasy. Neither of the superpowers would tolerate the dominance of the other and as a duopoly they lack the capacity to act consistently in concert or to share stably the world between them.

Leaving aside a moral revolution or an empire on earth we seem to find no candidates for political solutions to our deadly dilemma. But perhaps we have neglected something? That something it is all too easy to ignore because it seems so much part of the liberal conscience, a proposal for peace by a philosopher of the Enlightenment.

PERPETUAL PEACE

Kant's *On Perpetual Peace* can hardly be said to have been ignored, but it was, until recently, misread.[3] Kant was one of the pantheon of liberal intellectuals thought to be a 'precursor' of that misbegotten progeny of that marriage of nineteenth-century illusions and twentieth-century political cynicism – the League of Nations. *Perpetual Peace* is not an anticipation of 'collective security'; it is something else. But what? 'Collective security' could only be the use of force to preserve an unstable status quo, the world of the Versailles *diktat* or the Yalta carve-up.

It took a now deeply unpopular philosopher, besmirched with the stain of fascism, Carl Schmitt, to see the League of Nations for what it was. Schmitt's judgement is scathing: 'The Geneva League of Nations does not eliminate the possibility of wars, just as it does not abolish states. It introduces new possibilities for wars, permits wars to take place, sanctions coalition wars, and by legitimising and sanctioning certain wars it sweeps away many obstacles to war' (*Concept of the Political*, p. 56). Schmitt sees the moral duplicity in 'wars to end wars', in a league of armed states to preserve 'peace'. He denounces the pacifist vocabulary used to cloak the use of force to preserve an international 'order', to convert its opponents into '*hostis*', into outlaws and moral inferiors. Schmitt says:

> War is condemned but executions, punitive expeditions, pacifications, protection of treaties, international police, and measures to assure peace remain. The adversary is no longer called an enemy but a disturber of peace and is thereby designated an outlaw of humanity. A war waged to protect or expand economic power must, with the aid of propaganda, turn into a crusade and into the last war of humanity . . . But this allegedly non-political and apparently even antipolitical system serves existing or newly emerging friend-and-enemy groupings and cannot escape the logic of the political. (ibid., p. 79).

Schmitt spoke from the standpoint of the main loser in the Versailles *diktat*. He could show how the League, if taken seriously, sought to secure the world for the victors in 1918. It dismembered and economically subordinated Germany. The League was a hollow force – crippled by the isolationism of the United States, by the irresolution, cowardice and economic weakness of Britain and France. But had these powers been resolute, the League could only have been an alliance in defence of a world status quo, clothed in the language of high-minded morality. Resolution could only have led to a series of police actions against Germany, on the model of the French occupation of the Saar and Rhineland in 1923.

But Kant did not propose an alliance of armed states to 'keep the peace'. Kant's proposals exclude 'collective security', as we shall see. *Perpetual Peace* takes the form of a series of articles of an agreement between states. I shall outline Kant's articles and then comment on them. They are divided into preliminary and definitive articles.

Preliminary articles

1 'No treaty of peace shall be held valid in which there is tacitly reserved matter for a future war.'
2 'No independent state, large or small, shall come under the dominion of another state by inheritance, exchange, purchase or donation.'
3 'Standing armies shall in time be totally abolished.'
4 'National debts shall not be contracted with a view to the external friction of states.'
5 'No state shall by force interfere with another state.'
6 'No state shall, during war, permit such acts of hostility which would make mutual confidence in the subsequent peace impossible: such are the employment of assassins, poisoners, breach of capitulation, and incitement to treason in the opposing state.'

Articles 1, 5 and 6 are strict and must hold regardless of circumstances and immediately; articles 2, 3 and 4 are permissive and shall come into force gradually.

Definitive articles

1 'The Civil constitution of every state should be republican.'
2 'The law of nations shall be founded on a federation of free states.'
3 'The law of world citizenship shall be limited to conditions of universal hospitality.'

The language of Kant's proposed treaty may be antiquated and quaint, but it is extremely perceptive and, as one would expect from its author, has none of the cant of 'wars to end wars'. Kant proposes in article 1 that states settle existing differences, and that peace treaties shall be as close to genuine agreements as possible. Article 2 then freezes the status quo thus established. States must remain as they are, within their existing borders. Kant excludes 'peaceful' changes in the balance of power which might constitute a *casus belli*. Kant obviously and unspokenly excludes conquest and annexation. His list of prohibited methods of increasing the size of a state – inheritance, exchange, purchase or donation – relates to a pre-modern world of dynastic states. But the principle is clear and under modern conditions it would exclude – as part of an agreement – changes in borders based on 'the right of nations to self-determination'. Admitting such a principle would leave the system of states permanently open to change, since what constitutes a 'nation' is politically an open question.

Article 3 and article 6 show Kant's hostility to the very idea of 'collective security'. Permanent military forces are to be gradually abolished. Kant believed that dynastic states and mercenary armies perpetuated war. Like many liberals after him he could not imagine *popular* militarism. 1914 dented but did not destroy that illusion. It represented a lethal combination of demagogic mass politics, conscript armies, and military and political elites planning for war in a system of states characterized by an unstable balance of power. The spectacle of semi-militarized 'civilian' masses baying for war upset liberal hopes that war was the obsolete pastime of an aristocratic military caste. Kant's point stands nevertheless. He proposes militia forces sufficient only for self-defence. Each state has a guarantee against aggression and an instrument of defence which is difficult to use offensively to advantage. We no longer find our primary threat in 'armies' – in Kant's quaint Latin usage of *'miles perpetuus'*, men permanently under arms – but in missile forces ready for immediate use, requiring a response to attack faster than any political decision-making process. Article 6 enjoins states to settle differences by peaceful means, not 'collective security'. It says that *no* state shall interfere with another by force – for any reason. If war happens, it happens. It cannot be prevented by planning war against transgressors; such a collective-security treaty builds war into its articles rather than peace.

Articles 4 and 6 may appear old-fashioned. But that is because we have become used to the conditions prohibited therein as a part of what we choose to call 'peace'. The Superpowers and many lesser powers use assassins and incite treason as part of their normal espionage practices.

Kant's definitive articles involve the political changes necessary to make the preliminary articles work. By a 'republican' constitution Kant means a state which is a commonwealth, not an autocratic monarchy. A constitutional monarchy with a representative legislative assembly mould meet Kant's condition. His point is that the members of a commonwealth should have a say through their representatives in matters of peace and war. It may appear that most modern Western states meet this condition. Actually they do not. War has become a matter of delegated authority – the apparatus of state security is increasingly insulated from popular pressure and protected by a wall of secrecy. The realities of nuclear weapons have taken war out of the realm of political decision. For nuclear war to be subject to democratic control would involve radical changes in technology, in the control of information and in political structures. Kant's 'republican constitution' would involve considerable updating.

Article 2 involves Kant in a number of careful avoidances. He argues:

A state of peace, therefore, must be *established*, for in order to be secured against hostility it is not sufficient that hostilities simply be not committed; and, unless this security is pledged to each by his neighbour (a thing that can occur only in a civil state), each may treat his neighbour, from whom he demands this security, as an enemy. (*Perpetual Peace*, p. 92)

Kant follows Hobbes in treating the state of nature as a state of war. States remain in a state of nature *vis-à-vis* one another. The very idea of an analogous solution to the state of nature among states to that among men, a social contract in which they join together, is rejected. Men surrender their capacity under the state of nature to act in their own cause to a superior public power. States cannot or will not do this. States are not individuals and cannot surrender their capacity to act in their own cause, to make war, without ceasing to be states. States cannot behave in this way without contradiction – to do so is to cease to be sovereign public powers.

Kant sees no hope of a 'world republic'. Instead he proposes 'the negative surrogate of an alliance which averts war'. Kant's federation of free states is based on a mutual pledge that each will not attack the other. It involves not a social contract which establishes a superior public power, but a mutual pledge not to act in a certain way. The federation need not be universal, but a growing alliance of like-minded states which draws in others by their example and *not* by their collective force.

Kant unreservedly condemns an 'empire of the earth':

the idea of international law presupposes the separate existence of many independent but neighbouring states. Although this condition is itself a state of war (unless a federative union prevents the outbreak of hostilities), this is rationally preferable to the amalgamation of states under one superior power, as this would end in one universal monarchy, and laws always lose in vigour what government gains in extent; hence a soulless despotism falls into anarchy after stifling the seeds of good. (ibid., p. 113)

Kant's federation does not rely on goodwill or adherence to high ideals. Kant's view of humanity and of states is akin to that of Hobbes. But this does not cause him to despair. As he says: 'The problem of organising a state, however hard it may seem, can be solved even for a race of devils, if only they are intelligent' (ibid., p. 112). Men are *driven* to cooperate despite their inclinations and their differences, so are states. *Nature* is the great guarantor of the eventual reign of perpetual peace. Nature is not a benign goddess, a bloodless eighteenth-century creature. The very pressure of competition between states and the increasing costs of war force them to seek peace. The increasing interaction of states one with another and their growing commerce force them into more orderly relations. Finally, the differences of the human race, in language and religion, assure the survival of states and the failure of the enterprise of an 'empire of the earth'.

Kant does not imagine 'nature's' lesson will be quickly learnt or that wars will immediately cease to occur. His world of perpetual peace is not a world without politics or differences, it is a world in which states, like rational devils, have learned to keep political strife within their boundaries and to settle differences by means other than war. They are like shipwrecked sailors who agree to take turns in the water rather than fight over and capsize an overcrowded boat.[4]

But Schmitt claimed that: 'A world in which the possibility of war is utterly eliminated, a completely pacified globe, would be a world without the distinction of friend and enemy and hence a world without politics' (*Concept of the Political*, p. 35). This is not Kant's world, for the possibility of war is not utterly eliminated. On the contrary, Kant's world is a world of states and in it war is always at the very least possible. It is the very possibility of war, its cost and suffering, which is the spur to peace. Kant certainly limits by his treaty the emergence of the distinction of friend and enemy among states. He does not deny the existence of struggles or differences, but he implies that they constantly threaten peace and require that peace be established by deliberate policy. It is Schmitt's failing, not Kant's, to consider that friend–enemy relations define the political in a complete and exclusive way. Kant knows politics to be a realm in which human wills conflict but he denies that politics consists in nothing more than naked power struggles and the Machiavellian use of whatever means are available.

Kant's ideal is the 'moral politician': who seeks to bridge the realms of morality and political expediency; who neither has illusions about the world nor wallows in its evil.[5] The moral politician, acting in accordance with ethically sound maxims of conduct, has a consistent pattern of conduct. The Machiavellian pragmatist, who will use any means, suffers in consequence from a fatal heteronomy of action. Kant's motto for the moral politician is: 'By ye therefore wise as serpents – *and* – as harmless as doves.' A tall order, but not the view of a naive idealist. In certain circumstances neither wisdom nor pacific intent will suffice. Kant's moral politician must then either enter political struggle on the enemies' terms or abandon it altogether. Kant's advocacy of moral constancy, however, has roots outside of politics and ones that Kant is unwilling to surrender for merely prudential reasons. Kant's Pietist roots show through here. His moral politician is like Dürer's Knight – he persists, unshaken in his course, in a ruined world, oblivious to the blandishments of the Devil and the threat of Death.

THE ABOLITION

But what has this to do with nuclear weapons? Kant, as we have seen, avoided the pitfalls of pleading for world government or indulging in the war-perpetuating solution of 'collective security'. Kant might well regard his 'nature' as working rather well today. War between the major states of Europe is now unthinkable; commerce *has* replaced war, whereas only fifty years ago it was a looming threat. The Superpowers avoid direct conflict between themselves – they know the costs of war, even though they cannot agree on the shape of peace.

Kant wrote at a time when military technology posed no threat to peace, rather, bellicose leaders did. Today we cannot be so confident – Michael Howard notwithstanding.[6] Certainly neither of the Superpowers has a bellicose leadership like that of Hitler or even Wilhelm II. For all the mutual abuse, and for all the willingness to pound lesser states 'into the stone age', the Superpowers behave with profound caution in their dealings one with another. But each views the other's nuclear arsenal with nothing less than paranoia. 'Deterrence' is a political condition – it immobilizes the will to pursue policy by certain means – but it also rests on an unstable technical balance. The technology has inherent features which make mutual fear of a surprise attack a possible source of war.

Interestingly enough we have no need to 'update' Kant. This has been done for us, not by a modern philosopher nor by a strategic analyst, but by a journalist whose profound fear of nuclear weapons has made him think about the politics of peace with a clarity unmatched in the academy or the political parties. Jonathan Schell's *The Fate of the Earth* was an instant success. Actually it stated the obvious (the horrendous consequences of a large-scale nuclear war) in a laborious detail that would be unnecessary, were it not for the fact that some idiots in the undergrowth of the United States nuclear-policy industry appeared to think that such a war could be fought and won. It ended with what appeared to be a hint of a familiar political non-solution, world government.

The Fate of the Earth was politically unimpressive. Schell's more recent work *The Abolition* (1984) is quite the reverse. It is virtually a re-writing of *Perpetual Peace* to meet the conditions of the nuclear age. The author is apparently ignorant of Kant's political theory and his proposal for peace among states in particular.

Schell, now recognizes that world government is impossible and undesirable. To move from the state of nature, international anarchy, to a world civil state is undesirable because such a government would magnify all the evils of the 'sovereign power' we find in national states.

Schell realizes that the nation states' claim to a monopoly of violence does not necessarily lead to stable lawful authority which limits violence:

> Unfortunately, the centralisation of power does not necessarily require a shift from 'lawlessness' to 'law', as advocates of world government sometimes seem to suggest. The central authority can be, in a moral sense, as 'lawless' as any individual. When the central authority in question is a world government, this possibility assumes terrifying proportions, which have no precedent in the annals of politics . . . the prospect of a supreme political power ruling over the whole earth remains chilling. Anarchy is not liberty, yet it could be that in anarchy, with all its violence, the human spirit has greater latitude to live and grow than it would have in the uniform shadow of a global state. (*The Abolition*, pp. 95–6)

Schell, like Kant, recognizes that the opposition of a state of nature and a civil state is not the only option in international politics. Schell argues that nuclear weapons have led to a stalemate in the relations between the Superpowers. Deterrence has worked in the last four decades – 'worked' in the sense of having removed a major war as a policy option. Deterrence is not successful because it conforms to some theoretical doctrine, which both the Superpowers share. Deterrence is a primitive 'existential' condition. Deterrence, however, settles nothing. War, for all its evils, was a way of settling international issues, of enabling one policy rather than another to prevail. Deterrence is quite different to war, although it relies on the possession of hitherto unimagined military force. Insofar as deterrence works it persuades leaders not to act. Schell recognizes what has been obvious since Bernard Brodie's perceptive recognition of the implications of the atomic bomb. Nuclear weapons 'deter' their own use.[7] They terrify leaders into avoiding the policies which might lead others to their use against them.

Nuclear weapons have driven states out of the state of nature by radically restricting their possible courses of action. A state of deterrence has 'spoiled war – the final arbiter in the state of nature' (*The Abolition*, p. 97). Schell argues as follows: 'A deterred world . . . is no longer in anarchy – in the traditional state of nature. Nor, of course, is it in a civil state. It is . . . a new state altogether – the deterred state – which has been brought into being by the all-pervasive . . . reality of a nuclear-capable world' (ibid., p. 97). We no longer need to abolish war among the nuclear powers because our new techology has done it for us. Kant's 'nature' has made the costs of war impossible to sustain for any minimally rational leader. What we can do is to capitalize on the stalemate, the mutual immobilization of national policies, by a political agreement. As Bernard Brodie argued, the military fact of nuclear deterrence gives us the time to work out a viable alternative in politics.

No wonder *The Abolition* was not the massive success with the Peace Movement that *The Fate of the Earth* had been. It has been marginalized in both the USA and Europe. No nuclear disarmer could accept Schell's recognition of the deterred state. Schell, of course, does not believe that the deterred state, for all its immobilization of certain political options, is a stable one. We cannot remain in a pre-political 'existential' condition of deterrence. The reason is that we stand to lose everything in the unlikely, but possible, event that deterrence fails. However improbable, the consequences of the event are too serious to tolerate the risk of its occurring. We must therefore eliminate that risk by eliminating nuclear weapons.

Schell, like Kant, recognizes that there is a price to be paid for instituting perpetual peace. Disarmament must be an agreement between states and, therefore, must take account of the interests of those states. Peace is not a revolutionary objective, but a profoundly conservative one. This is perhaps another reason for the lack of interest of the part of CND. Schell proposes a 'first step' which is daring in the context of US rhetoric and policy – 'to accept the political verdict that has been delivered by deterrence, and formalise the stalemate' (*The Abolition*, p. 110). That means foregoing policy aims which have become a delusion in a deterred state, such as 'rollback' in Eastern Europe. They *have* been abandoned, except *as* delusions. Schell proposes accepting the *de facto* settlement as one 'in principle'. This means to accept, 'our present world, with all its injustices and other imperfections, as our ideal, and then seek the most sensible and moderate means of preserving it' (ibid., p. 111). Kant's preliminary articles 2 and 5 are modified to suit the post-Yalta world. Non-interference must inevitably involve the recognition of the Superpowers' *de facto* empires and the mutual acceptance of spheres of influence. It involves removing all 'reserved business', settling areas of conflict and mutual competition – in Africa, Asia and the Middle East. A deal of this kind is easier to comprehend for Russian and European foreign policy makers, and more acceptable to their populations, than it is to US politicians and sections of the US populace. It is also difficult to comprehend for many members of CND and END, who see peace as a left-wing and liberating cause. Peace can only be acceptable to the most powerful states if it respects their interests, which are profoundly unrevolutionary.

However, such a settlement still presupposes being able to deal with nuclear weapons. Can a disarmed world retain the properties of a deterred world, but without its threat of immediate destruction? How can we abolish nuclear weapons when we can never forget or unlearn the technology which produced them? Schell answers these questions in reverse order and thereby resolves the contradiction they seem to pose.

We cannot unlearn nuclear technology. But Schell makes the continued existence of nuclear weapon-producing capacity a strong rather than a crippling feature of nuclear disarmament. Schell's argument is ingenious. A post-nuclear world remains a deterred world in that the actions of the powers are constrained by a continuing balance, that of the threat of nuclear re-armament. Both of the Superpowers would retain a carefully monitored and inspected capacity to re-introduce nuclear weapons. This would allow either to re-arm in a matter of weeks, in sufficient time to prevent the opposition from overturning the stalemate. The advantage is that deterrence still exists but the nuclear 'fuse' is lengthened to the point that it permits states to subject nuclear weapons to political control. It enables us to undo the disastrous hair trigger which gives the nuclear-security apparatuses virtual political autonomy and thus to permit political control without very radical changes in the political machinery of the Superpowers.[8]

In that sense, disarmament makes possible 'republican' government. Neither the USA nor the USSR are to be considered models of such government; even if both formally posses a representative legislative assembly which delegates executive authority. In the USA, as has been said, 40 per cent of the electorate fails to vote even in Presidential elections and only the very wealthy can hope to seek major office. In the USSR, until 1989, the electorate could only acclaim the pre-selected candidates of the one officially recognized Party and the Supreme Soviet was a creature of that Party's government. The new reforms have barely scratched the surface of one-party rule in the Soviet Union. In neither country, however, is the Government uninfluenced by or indifferent to the aspirations of the populace in the matter of peace. The vast majority of both populations desire peace and abhor war, and both Governments claim, and I believe most of their leading members are sincere in this, that they will never start a nuclear war. By and large the mud that both sides' hired publicists fling at one another sticks and with good reason: the USA *is* close to being a capitalist plutocracy and the USSR *does* display aspects of a police state. But neither has complete contempt for the aspirations of their people. Even if we may heartily detest aspects of the institutions and policies of both states, we cannot assume some abstract and unlikely-to-be-realized ideal of democratic government as a precondition for peace. On the contrary, peace and political agreement between the Superpowers are a precondition for greater democratization in both of them and in some of their satellites and clients.

Kant doesn't look quite so antiquated after all. But, for disarmament and a political settlement to be possible, do the leaders of the Superpowers have to be as wise as serpents in order to see the need to be as harmless as doves? One hopes not – at least they need be no cleverer if a little better than Henry Kissinger. A settlement would be a rough-and-ready affair, subject to conflict and tension, to reversals and defeats for each Power in its sphere of influence, and it would inevitably involve some undecided issues and even some 'reserved business'. Nuclear peace, precisely because its foundations are conservative, will not rest on some new international order of amity and concord. The world of the Yalta *diktat*, revised by forty years of struggle, is a world of injustice and unsettled issues.

Here Schell's weaknesses begin to show. Schell's argument is ingenious, and it shows us our best hope for a feasible nuclear peace. It is written from the viewpoint of a well-off American who wants peace in order to enjoy the good things of life, and without the nagging fear that it might all end one night. A Palestinian refugee or a Polish miner, a Salvadorian or an Afghan peasant, an Iranian Muslim fundamentalist or a black militant in South Africa, may not see it in this way. Schell may reply that nuclear war destroys all hopes, all aspirations. But to many people the threats to them consequent upon the Superpowers consolidating the present international order are for more immediate than the unlikely but possible dangers of nuclear war. Perhaps that order is already in ruins and the Superpowers weary titans so distracted by their efforts to preserve hegemony in their crumbling informal empires that all hope of an agreement between them is long past. If so, the prospects for nuclear peace are grim. In fact, although the world has become more mutli-polar than in the 1950s and examples of open defiance of the Superpowers can easily be found, the political options for minor powers are still limited to local and politically containable challenges to hegemony. Given an agreement between the Superpowers, such challenges could be met more easily by each of them and no minor power has the capacity to sabotage such an agreement, not even Israel.

Schell fails to notice that his post-nuclear world, as a deterred world, suffers from many of the paradoxes of deterrence, even though it does not have the weapons that appear to give rise to them. The lengthening of the nuclear 'fuse' increases the contradictions involved in deterrence, in that all that is prevented by deterrence is the use of nuclear weapons. It sharpens some of the contradictions, for example, how to respond to a provocation or conventional defeat? To re-arm and threaten to use nuclear weapons? We are familiar with the paradox that nuclear weapons, primed and available, cannot be used to pursue conventional policy goals and cannot compensate for conventional military weakness. To take the classic scenario for such a paradox, assume a crisis in which the USSR were to launch a pre-emptive conventional attack on Western Europe, defeat the US forces, and occupy the territory of the Federal Republic of Germany. What could the US do? Launch a nuclear attack? Or, if disarmed, assemble the bomb and then use it?

What an effective parity of nuclear weapons does is to prevent their

possessors using them against one another or persuing strategies that
threaten nuclear war, supposing minimal rationality. It might even be
argued that it is the very over-abundance of nuclear weapons and the
very 'short fuse' which keeps the Superpowers from conventional
adventures. Lengthen the fuse and one increases the paradox of
deterrence, and, therefore, reduces the risk involved in conventional
adventures and the creation of crises in pursuit of foreign policy.
Perhaps the result would be to resurrect forms of 'policy' that require
certain means for their continuation. The answer to this paradox is no
different in either state of the deterred world, full nuclear armament or
complete nuclear disarmament. Nuclear peace and perpetual peace are
not the same thing. Nuclear peace prevents the end of all things but it
does not assure all peace. The paradox of nuclear stalemate can only be
met by a policy of conventional deterrence, increasing the probability
that conventional adventures will be met by sufficient conventional
force. Such a policy is very expensive and is resisted in Western Europe
for that reason. Nevertheless, it is the likely price to be paid for
complete nuclear disarmament.[9]

Conventional re-armament may be the consequence of nuclear disarmament. Not only in Western Europe, but also for the USSR against
China and for the USA for purposes of counter-insurgency in the Third
World. This is even on the assumption of a measure of detente. Nuclear
disarmament presupposes detent, but even given a willingness to disarm
and settle differences the Superpowers will seek military reassurance.
The problem is that it is probably easier to agree on nuclear disarmament than on the level of conventional armaments both Superpowers
would feel necessary to preserve the status quo.

It would be surprising if any private peace proposal were without
faults. Schell's argument reveals its political priorities; its ingenuity is
matched by its author's blindness. It is, however, possible, in the way
world government or a moral revolution on the part of the leaders of the
Superpowers are not.

Notes

NOTES TO CHAPTER 1

1 I have developed this point about the limits parliamentary democracy imposes upon socialism at greater length in 'Democracy, Socialism's Best Reply to the Right' in Barry Hindess (ed.), *Reactions to the Right* (1990).

2 See Boris Frankel, *The Post-Industrial Utopians* (1988).

3 I have critically assessed the 'new republicanism' in chapter 2 of *After Thatcher?* (1989). A good summary of the new republican ideas on citizenship is to be found in Chantal Mouffe, 'The Civics Lesson', *New Statesman and Society* (1988) and in Stuart Hall and David Held, 'Left and Rights', *Marxism Today* (1989). A good discussion of the 'civil society' approach is to be found in John Keane, *Democracy and Civil Society* (1988).

4 See Harold J. Laski, 'The Problem of Administrative Areas' in Paul Hirst (ed.), *The Pluralist Theory of the State* (1989).

5 A selection of the key writings of Cole, Laski and Figgis is to be found in Hirst (ed.), *The Pluralist Theory of the State*.

6 I have developed this point about the necessity of a social pact more fully in *After Thatcher?*

7 The importance of regional economies and local and regional economic regulation is emphasized in several of the papers in Paul Hirst and Jonathan Zeitlin (eds), *Reversing Industrial Decline?* (1988).

8 I have tried to counter the fashionable thesis of the breakdown of Superpower hegemony in chapter 9 of this book and more specifically tried to argue against the thesis of the collapse of American hegemony in chapter 3 of *After Thatcher?*

9 This argument is clearly very unpopular with CND and the peace movement generally: hostility to the thesis that disarmament and detente are essentially conservative processes which modify but do not undermine the present international system is at the root of Peter Behr's critical response to the paper which forms chapter 9 of this book; see Behr, 'Peace and Political Theory: A Reply to Paul Hirst', *Economy and Society* (1989) and my response in the same issue.

10 I have discussed the Labour leadership's hostility to Charter 88 in particular and political reform in general in chapter 2 of *After Thatcher?*

NOTES TO CHAPTER 2

First published in *The Political Quarterly*, vol. 59 no. 2, April–June 1988.

1 I have discussed the concept of 'political mechanism' and the wider issue of the democratic reform of British Government in 'Extending Democracy', chapter 5 of *Law, Socialism and Democracy* (1986).
2 See Max Weber, *Economy and Society*, vol. III, p. 951 (1969).
3 See his 'Lectures on Civic Morals' in *Professional Ethics and Civic Morals* (1957).
4 For a positive account of corporatism in the economic policies of certain European states like Austria and Sweden, see Peter J. Katzenstein, *Small States in World Markets* (1985).
5 See Williams et al., 'Facing Up to Manufacturing Failure' in Hirst and Zeitlin (eds), *Reversing Industrial Decline?*
6 See Paul Hirst, 'The Politics of Industrial Policy', in ibid.

NOTES TO CHAPTER 3

First published in W. Outhwaite and M. Mulkay (eds), *Social Theory and Social Criticism: Essays Presented to T. B. Bottomore*, Oxford: Basil Blackwell (1987).

1 The analysis of power in terms of three dimensions is taken from Steven Lukes, *Power, A Radical View* (1974). This paper is not concerned with the concept of 'power' as such, however, it is worth pointing out that 'three-dimensional' accounts of power can be radically different one from another. Dahl, as will be seen below, is quite capable of explaining power relations in terms of two- and three-dimensional accounts – the three dimensions should not be taken as more than an expository device nor should one imagine Dahl is actually as 'one-dimensional' as he is presented in expositions or as some of his own remarks suggest. I have taken the three dimensions as they stand for purposes of exposition and have not enquired further into the defects of 'capacity-outcome' views of power. For a discussion of the concept of power which is highly critical of conventional views see Barry Hindess, 'Power, Interests and the Outcomes of Struggles', *Sociology* (1982): see also his critical discussion of 'interests' 'Rational Choice Theory end the Analysis of Political Action', *Economy and Society* (1984). Likewise, I have, also for purposes of exposition, largely accepted conventional views of the concepts of 'class', 'class interests' and 'ruling class' because my point is that even on their own terms most Marxist accounts of ruling-class power are defective and themselves raise the need for some form of account like the pluralist theory of democratic political competition.

2 Which is not to say most serious pluralists have been right wing, merely that in political – intellectual debate pluralism was used in this manner and castigated as such on the left.

3 John Burnheim's *Is Democracy Possible?* (1985) is an interesting example of a radical criticism of contemporary representative democracy, which uses Dahl's analysis as one of its starting points, and then goes on to suggest an alternative which would be a direct democracy. Burnheim's proposal is 'demarchy', the rule of members of the general public to run the affairs of the multiple organizations in a stateless society on the basis of selection by lot.

4 Which is not to say that pluralism is beyond criticism or that polyarchy is a sufficient basis for a theory of an adequately democratic polity. I have raised the value of pluralism sharply and polemically here because of the degree of misunderstanding almost universal on the left. I have also stressed some very pessimistic conclusions for the left which arise from a pluralist analysis: a pluralist view of contemporary politics does not mean that the left will have an equal chance of influence in decision-making along with everyone else; far from it. Pluralism helps to show *why* democratic socialism is so difficult to attain. In *Law, Socialism and Democracy*, I have discussed the need for the political reforms if greater democratization is to be attained and the limits of the polyarchical view of democracy. In that work I have also considered the political deilemmas of democratic socialism in more depth than is possible here.

NOTES TO CHAPTER 4

First published in *The Journal of Law and Society*, special issue on 'Critical Legal Studies', vol. 14 no. 1, Spring 1987.

A word of explanation is necessary for the somewhat telegraphic tone of this paper. In some ways it is an 'internal document', a polemical contribution to the debate on how the British critical legal studies movement should develop. The movement towards criticism of intellectual and professional orthodoxy in law on the part of legal academics and radical practitioners has developed since the 1970s in Britain, France and the USA. Each movement is different. The American began strongly with an 'internal critique' of law, measuring its concepts and supposed standards against its practice and consequences. The French group *Critique du Droit* began with a more explicitly Marxist orientation. CLS developed in Britain in the early 1980s and was institutionalized with the creation of the Critical Legal Conference in 1984. British CLS is much less coherent than were the American and the French movements when they began, although they too are now more varied. Given that tendency toward continuous debate, the intellectual orientation of British CLS is hard to define and can best be sampled by looking at the special issue of the *Journal of Law and Society* noted above, which has also been reprinted as a book, Peter Fitzpatrick and Alan Hunt (eds) *Critical Legal Studies* (1987). For a more comprehensive account of the American CLS movement see: Mark Kelman, *A Guide to Critical Legal Studies* (1987).

1 Kirchheimer's views from the Weimar Period on into the 1950s are to be found in his collected essays entitled *Politics, Law and Social Change*, ed. F. S. Burin and K. L. Shell (1969). Neumann's views on the necessity of a liberal-democratic political and legal order are likewise to be found in his collected essays entitled *The Democratic and the Authoritarian State* (1957). See also Neumann's *The Rule of Law* (1986) and a collection of Kirchheimer and Neumann's Weimar essays, Keith Tribe (ed.), *Social Democracy and the Rule of Law* (1987).

2 There is a massive literature on the varieties of pluralist theories of the state. Pluralism is discussed more fully in chs 5 and 7. D. Nicholls, *The Pluralist State* (1975) offers an able exposition of English pluralism, centred on J. N. Figgis. Figgis's most impressive and relevant work is *Churches in the Modern State* (1913). For Maitland see his 'Introduction' to Otto von Gierke, *Political Theories of the Middle Age* (1900) and for a thorough account of von Gierke himself see J. D. Lewis, *The Genossenschaft Theory of Otto von Gierke* (1935).

3 The classic statement of H. L. A. Hart's position is to be found in *The Concept of Law* (1961).

4 Schmitt was a critic of the pluralist theory of the state; his strictures are telling against G. D. H. Cole and H. J. Laski but are less so against Figgis.

5 See John Austin, *The Province of Jurisprudence Determined* (1832).

6 For a fuller discussion of this point see Hirst, *Law, Socialism and Democracy*, ch. 2, pp. 16–27.

7 See G. D. H. Cole, *Guild Socialism Re-Stated* (1920) and *The Social Theory* (1920).

8 See Burnheim, *Is Democracy Possible?*

9 See Chen Erjin, *China, Crossroads Socialism* (1984).

NOTES TO CHAPTER 5

First published in *The Journal of Law and Society*, special issue on 'Law, Democracy and Social Justice', vol. 15 no. 1, Spring 1988.

1 On the decline of workerist socialism see Andre Gorz *Farewell to the Working Class* (1982).

2 What is striking about most of these facts, trumpeted by the prophets of 'postmodernism' and the heralds of 'new times', are that they were seen at least in outline by Eduard Bernstein in his *Evolutionary Socialism* published at the very end of the last century.

3 This whole issue of associationalist socialism and its defeat by social democracy is covered more fully in chapter 6. Associational socialism has been represented by a number of movements and currents of ideas, for example, English Guild Socialism, the experiments inspired by Morris and the English Arts and Crafts Movement, the French mutualist tradition influenced by Proudhon, the various cooperative movements, and so on. G. D. H. Cole's *A History of Socialist Thought* (1953–61) attempts to do justice to this complex tradition, unlike the triumphalist histories written by

some Social Democrats and Bolsheviks. Anthony Wright's *Socialisms* (1986) is a much shorter but excellent essay in the same vein. The best short work on Guild Socialism is S. T. Glass, *The Responsible Society* (1966); on Proudhon and the French tradition see Steven Vincent, *Pierre-Joseph Proudhon and the Origins of French Republican Socialism* (1984); on the arts and crafts movement and its social experiments see Helen Irving, 'Romanticism and British Socialism: Art and Work in Socialist Thought 1889–1920' (1986); see also Stephen Yeo, 'Three Socialisms: Statism, Collectivism and Associationalism' in William Outhwaite and Michael Mulkay (eds), *Social Theory and Social Criticism* (1987).

4 I have developed this argument about why a plurality of realms of agencies of decision requires a legal order and a distinct public power in chapter 4 above and in *Law, Socialism and Democracy*, ch. 2.

5 Figgis is one of the most important and most neglected political thinkers in twentieth-century Britain. He understood both the need to challenge centralized 'sovereign' states *and* the need for a public power and a legal order, unlike many other critics who tend toward either anarchism or incoherence. The plenitude of power implied in the granting of sovereignty to a definite political body is pernicious and unnecessary, quite different from that primacy of certain rules necessary to the public power in a pluralist state. That primacy is regulatory and limited by its function, the pluralist state is *not* a total state, on the contrary it cedes most substantive functions to self-governing associations freely formed of citizens. The problem is that Figgis never wrote an extensive political treatise outlining these views. Nicholls, *The Pluralist State* is the best exposition of Figgis's ideas.

6 I have discussed the nature of pluralism as a political theory more fully in the Introduction to Hirst (ed.), *The Pluralist Theory of the State*. This work contains selections from the works of G. D. H. Cole, J. N. Figgis and H. J. Laski, including the bulk of Cole's *Social Theory*, a key chapter from Figgis's *Churches in the Modern State* and Laski's 'The Problem of Administrative Areas' from Laski, *The Foundations of Sovereignty and Other Essays* (1921).

7 Free Church of Scotland Appeals – discussed in Figgis, *Churches in the Modern State*, pp. 18–22.

8 See chapter 3 above.

9 For the concept of 'liberal collectivism' see Cutler et al., *Keynes, Beveridge and Beyond* (1986).

10 I have tried to show how at least the beginnings of associationalism and pluralism could be related to practical politics in *After Thatcher?*

NOTES TO CHAPTER 6

An abridged version of this piece appeared in the *New Statesman*, 6 March 1987, in a special issue devoted to the future of Socialism.

1 Bernstein's arguments appeared in developed form in 1899 and the English translation entitled *Evolutionary Socialism* appeared in 1909.

2 For an analysis of the failure of British manufacturing see Karel Williams et

al., *Why are the British Bad at Manufacturing?* (1983); Cutler et al., *Keynes, Beveridge and Beyond*; and Keith Smith, *The British Economic Crisis* (1984).

3 See Rosa Luxemburg, *The Russian Revolution and Leninism or Marxism?* (1961) and Karl Kautsky, *The Dictatorship of the Proletariat* (1964).

4 If one doubts this, consult the work of a Russian and a Marxist, Roy Medvedev's *Let History Judge* (1972). It will not do in mitigation to say Stalin was popular or that the Soviet Union won great victories under his leadership during the 1941–5 War. The same, shamefully, can be said of Hitler; he too was popular and many Germans fought and died willingly not merely for their country, but for him.

5 Again, if this be doubted, read the thorough accounts written from the left: Moshe Lewin's *Russian Peasants and Soviet Power* (1968) and Teodor Shanin's *The Awkward Class* (1972).

6 For a careful attempt to assess the prospects for reform in the Soviet Union see Anthony Barnett, *Soviet Freedom* (1988).

7 For Proudhon see Vincent, *P. J. Proudhon* and for Cole see A. W. Wright, *G. D. H. Cole and Socialist Democracy* (1979).

8 The difficulty is that for so long socialism has been identified with the vision of a 'new society'. Marxists and non-Marxists alike believed in this singular future and that such a new society could be organized on the basis of a uniform institutional principle, such as the public or social ownership of the means of production, distribution and exchange. Abandoning this simplistic view of society involves accepting the institutional complexity of any conceivable form of social organization and the existence of a plurality of political interests and projects within it. If the illusions of 'totality' and of a necessary future are abandoned then socialists will have to learn to *start* from the principle that they will have to compete with and cooperate with non-socialist political forces, not as a tactic but for ever. For a valuable attempt to batter this lesson home against the illusions of classical Leninism, see A. J. Polan, *Lenin and the End of Politics* (1984).

9 This point is developed in chapter 2 above.

10 Most histories of socialism are either extremely partizan or academic. Of all the voluminous literature on the history of socialism, one short book stands out for its attempt to learn from past failures and address the future, Anthony Wright's *Socialisms*.

NOTES TO CHAPTER 7

Part of the first section of this chapter was published under the title 'Carl Schmitt's Decisionism' in a special issue of the journal *Telos* entitled *Carl Schmitt: Enemy or Foe?*, no. 72, Summer 1987.

1 I have chosen not to consider the English pluralists here since they are discussed elsewhere in this volume, notably chapters 4 and 5, and because I have written extensively on them in Hirst (ed.), *The Pluralist Theory of the*

State. Duguit's ideas, in contrast, have been little explored in English in recent years.

2 Carl Schmitt's work is beginning to be accessible to the non-German reader. In addition to the works on Schmitt in translation cited in this chapter and the next (all of which contain valuable introductions) there are now two English-language books on Schmitt which discuss his political and legal ideas and his political activities: George Schwab, *The Challenge of the Exception: An Introduction to the Political Ideas of Carl Schmitt between 1921 and 1936* (1970) and J. W. Bendersky, *Carl Schmitt, Theorist for the Reich* (1983). Two articles by F. R. Cristi, 'Hayek and Schmitt on the Rule of Law', *Canadian Journal of Political Science* (1984) and G. L. Ulmen, 'The Sociology of the State: Carl Schmitt and Max Weber', *State, Culture and Society* (1986), pt I, analyse Schmitt in relation to F. A. von Hayek and Max Weber respectively. In addition there is the *Telos* special issue on Schmitt noted above.

3 Schmitt was thoroughly familiar with the work of the English pluralists and also highly critical of them. His criticisms of Cole, Laski, etc., amount to this: that they view the state formally as an administrative machinery and then seek to decentralize it and distribute its tasks to a plurality of lesser functionally specific associations. This is to restore the depoliticizations characteristic of liberalism, but in the service of a new anti-political idea. For Schmitt, on the contrary, the state is a concrete political association in conflict with others which demands and receives loyalty, and such national political associations are inevitable in the modern world. Thus Schmitt claims that Cole, in particular, simply does not comprehend the political and tends to treat associations as matters of individual choice and convenience as to whether or not to join, as matters of chosen association. Schmitt's criticisms are to be found in *Concept of the Political* (pp. 39–45) and in 'Staatsethik und pluralisticher Staat', *Positionen und Begriffe im Kampf mit Weimar-Genf-Versailles* (1930) – I am grateful to G. L. Ulmen for drawing my attention to the latter reference.

   Schmitt's relation to continental pluralist jurisprudence was by no means as negative as his critique of the English. Schmitt had a high opinion of Maurice Hauriou's work and respected Duguit, largely because both were enemies of conventional liberalism, of legal positivism and of methodological formalism in the theory of law. I have been unable to consider Hauriou here because his work is so different from and in competition with Duguit that to explicate the relationship would require another paper and because I am not at all clear that Hauriou *was* in any meaningful sense a 'pluralist'.

4 Discussions of Dukheim abound – J. E. S. Hayward, 'Solidarist Syndicalism: Durkheim and Duguit', *Sociological Review* (1960), pt I; J. Neyer, 'Individualism and Socialism in Durkheim', in K. H. Wolff (ed.), *Emile Durkheim*, Essays on Sociology and Philosophy (1960); and M. Richter, 'Durkheim's Politics and Political Theory', in Wolff (ed.), *Emile Durkheim*. (1960) are particularly valuable and informative on Durkheim's political theory and his views on guilds. See also Frank Pearce, *Radical Durkheim* (1989). A. Black, *Guilds and Civil Society in European Political Thought from the Twelfth Century to the Present* (1984) sets Durkheim in a long history of corporatist thinking; for a critical evaluation of Black's book see Helen Irving,

'Guilds, Corporations and Socialist Theory', *Economy and Society* (1986). Duguit's jurisprudence is discussed in Hayward, 'Solidarist Syndicalism', pt II; Hsiao, *Political Pluralism*; H. J. Laski, *Authority in the Modern State* (1919); and Julius Stone, 'Two Theories of the Institution', in R. A. Newman (ed.), *Essays in Honour of Roscoe Pound* (1973), among others.

My discussion of Durkheim and Duguit is selective in the extreme and is not intended to cover all aspects of their theories. In particular it neglects Durkheim's concept of 'collective consciousness' and its use by Duguit as a foundation for this theory of law as an instrument of social organization. Ideas can be interesting in spite of their supposed theoretical foundations. It is a rationalistic error to suppose allegedly more 'basic' concepts or methodological doctrines determine the value and consequences of the whole of the theoretical writing in which they are found. I have discussed and criticized Durkheim's concept of the 'collective consciousness' in *Durkheim, Bernard and Epistemology* (1975) – it is only fair to add that the latter is by no means wholly free of that rationalistic error. Also, it should be noted, only one aspect of Duguit's public law doctrine is presented here and his views on private law are largely ignored.

NOTES TO CHAPTER 8

First published in *Economy and Society*, vol. 17 no. 2, May 1988.

1 Edward N. Luttwak's *Strategy: The Logic of War and Peace* (1987) sets out in a way unmatched since Clausewitz why strategy is governed by the fact that reciprocal action is dominant in war. Military action is ultimately governed by the need to match or to anticipate the moves of the enemy. War is simply an extreme case of a whole class of competitive processes, of which politics in Schmitt's sense is also a member. Any process of competition, that is not controlled and limited by norms subscribed to by the parties entering into it, is characterized by reciprocal action.
2 See chapter 9 below, where *Perpetual Peace* is again discussed, with a slightly different emphasis.
3 The phrase 'economy of violence' is the key to Sheldon Wolin's interpretation of Machiavelli in *Politics and Vision* (1961).
4 In his interpretation of the Nazi state, *Behemoth* (1942).
5 See Barry Hindess, 'Liberty and Equality' and Jim Tomlinson 'Market Socialism' in Hindess (ed.), *Reactions*.

NOTES TO CHAPTER 9

First published in *Economy and Society*, vol. 16 no. 2, May 1987.

1 On the liberal conscience see Michael Howard, *War and the Liberal Conscience* (1981).

2 Dahl, *After the Revolution?*, argues persuasively why a democratic world
   government is an absurd idea, but he also offers the prospect of something
   less appalling than an 'empire of the earth' for settling international issues
   outside the competence of individual sovereign states: 'It is hard for me to
   conceive how a "world democracy" could be made more oppressive and
   stultifying than by having it consist of nothing but elections and a representative body on one side, and a cabinet and bureaucracies on the other. Let your
   mind play for a moment with the thought of a World Minister of Education
   regulating your schools . . .' (ibid., p. 90). Dahl's answer is to accept the need
   for a hierarchy of institutions, each with political mechanisms appropriate to
   its level of competence. Such international issues could only be dealt with by
   inter-governmental agencies given 'delegated authority' and regulated by
   states.
3 For accounts of *Perpetual Peace* which patiently reconstruct its arguments and
   undo the long history of misreading see W. B. Gallie, *Philisophers of Peace
   and War* (1978) and F. H. Hinsley, *Power and the Pursuit of Peace* (1967). For
   a persuasive general summary of Kant's political theory see Howard Williams,
   Kant's Political Philosophy (1983).
4 Although he was not a pacifist, Kant regarded war as an abomination. Hegel's
   attitude to war was entirely different and he strongly condemned Kant's
   enterprise as a direct consequence of this attitude. In his *Philosophy of Right*
   (1967), Hegel endorsed the anarchy inevitable in a system of competing
   sovereign states as a healthy component in historical progress: 'War has the
   higher significance that by its agency . . . the ethical health of peoples is
   preserved in their indifference to the stabilisation of finite institutions; just as
   the blowing of winds preserves the sea from the foulness which would be the
   result of a prolonged calm, so also corruption in nations would be the product
   of prolonged, let alone "perpetual" peace'. (*Philosophy of Right*, p. 210).
   We can understand far better Kant's willingness to strive for the 'stabilisation of finite institutions', having full knowledge of the horrors of modern
   war. Hegel's attitude stems from an historicism in which world historic
   peoples could only be held back by any shallow ethical regard for the rights or
   lives of their inferiors. He justifies 'civilised nations . . . regarding and treating
   as barbarians those who lay behind them in institutions which are the essential
   moments of the state' (ibid., p. 219). This brutal endorsement of imperialism-
   as-progress is an attitude of mind Kant rightly regarded as abhorent. In
   Perpetual Peace he denounced the mentality of imperialism, attacking the
   civilized states of the world for, 'the injustice which they show to the lands and
   peoples they visit' which demonstrated 'they counted the inhabitants as
   nothing' (*Perpetual Peace*, pp. 103–4). The Great Powers have yet to learn the
   lesson and a world stabilized under their influence and control will remain
   brutal and problematic until the 'civilized' peoples lose this imperialist
   mentality.
   Hegel, normally an acute critic of other philosophers, simply did not
   understand *Perpetual Peace*. He (*Philosophy of Right*, pp. 213–14, 295–6)
   treats Kant as a narrow proponent of 'collective security' rather than someone
   who sought to challenge the mentality of authoritarianism and offensive war.
   Hegel simply cannot understand how it would be possible for states to forgo
   war as an aim of policy because his philosophy of history sees war as a

progressive force. Kant's philosophy of history accords war a place but neither a moral legitimacy nor an ultimate necessity.

5 For an account of Kant's concept of the 'moral politician' and his attempt to bridge morality and expediency in politics see Williams, *Kant's Political Philosophy*, ch. 2.

6 See 'The Causes of Wars' in M. Howard, *The Causes of War* (1983) his argument against naive views that nuclear wars can be started by accident or as a result of the arms race. His position makes sense until one tries to imagine the present very unstable international system and the present form of 'hair-trigger' deterrence continuing *ad infinitum*. Geoffrey Barraclough's *From Agadir to Armageddon* (1982) argues persuasively that the present international system can lead to crises which have war as an unintended consequence and that nuclear technology further increases that risk. It is naive to imagine that nuclear weapons are under firm *political* control: the command and control technology for nuclear weapons currently puts great weight on rapid decisions by senior military officers and heads of state. One need not suppose them to be bellicist or bloodthirsty to see how political tension could well lead to errors of judgement. One must also see that those judgements cannot be corrected by the opinions of democratic representatives or even the counsel of most members of a ministerial cabinet. Major operational security decisions are made by small and confidential committees, at best.

7 For an account of Brodie's views in the immediate post-War era see L. Freedman, *The Evolution of Nuclear Strategy* (1981), ch. 3. Brodie claimed: 'Thus far the chief purpose of a military establishment has been to win wars. From now on its chief purpose must be to avert them. It can have no other useful purpose' (cited in ibid., p. 44).

8 Schell has also made himself unpopular with the Peace Movement by supporting the Strategic Defense Initiative (SDI). For Schell, SDI would further guarantee a disarmed state by setting a virtually impossible threshold for an opponent who attempted to re-arm by stealth. SDI technology would defeat the small number of weapons which could be produced in secret and a larger number would take such an effort to produce that it would be discovered and counter-measures could be initiated before it was completed.

The mainstream public relations effort for SDI argues 'that it will make nuclear weapons obsolete without disarmament'. This is, of course, absurd and Schell has no part in this. SDI is, quite simply, technically unfeasible as a 'shield' against nuclear missiles in any numbers and it admits of many simple counter-measures. SDI is undoubtedly destabilizing, in the same way as a more conventional anti-missile rocket system would be. The Superpowers were right to conclude an anti-ABM agreement as part of the regularization of deterrence and the Soviet Union perceives SDI, in consequence, as a threat to the stability of deterrence and, therefore, to peace. For this reason, even if it were to be possible and to have merits in the event of nuclear disarmament, support for SDI must work against disarmament. On the technological problems of SDI see H. A. Bethe et al., 'Space-based Ballistic Missile Defence', *Scientific American* (1984).

9 Conventional deterrence is certainly no more stable than nuclear deterrence

and, while less disastrous if it fails, still involves threatening widespread destruction and the wholesale slaughter of the innocent. Conventional war may pale beside the horrors of a large-scale use of nuclear weapons but it is still repellent. A conventional war in Western Europe would convert Germany and much of Poland into a charnel house. 'Conventional' weapons have evolved in lethality since 1945 almost as much as their more sinister fellows. Only a fool would regard conventional 're-armament' with less than utter loathing. Some of the 'alternative defence' proposals emanating from the left are foolish, militarily ignorant and morally ugly. We cannot contrast cheap and cheerful 'defensive' weapons to expensive and frightful nuclear weapons: 'defensive' weapons – such as precision-guided munitions – are expensive and designed to kill and maim. For an informed discussion of the problems of conventional deterrence see ESECS, *Strengthening Conventional Deterrence in Europe* (1983).

Bibliography

Austin, John (1832) *The Province of Jurisprudence Determined*, intro. H. L. A. Hart (1954) London: Weidenfeld & Nicholson.

Bachrach, Peter and Morton Baratz (1962) 'Two Faces of Power', *American Political Science Review*, vol. 56, Dec., 947–52.

Barnett, Anthony (with Nella Bielski) (1988) *Soviet Freedom*, London: Pan Books.

Barraclough, G. (1982) *From Agadir to Armageddon*, London: Weidenfeld & Nicholson.

Behr, P. (1988) 'Peace and Political Theory: A Reply to Paul Hirst', *Economy and Society*, vol. 17 no. 1.

Bendersky, J. W. (1983) *Carl Schmitt, Theorist for the Reich*, Princeton NJ: Princeton University Press.

Bernstein, Eduard (1899) *Evolutionary Socialism*, New York: Schocken Books (1961).

Bethe, H. A. et al. (1984) 'Space-based Ballistic Missile Defence', *Scientific American*, vol. 251 no. 4, 37–47.

Black, A. (1984) *Guilds and Civil Society in European Political Thought from the Twelfth Century to the Present*, London: Methuen.

Bobbio, Noberto (1987) *The Future of Democracy*, Cambridge: Polity.

Burnheim, John (1985) *Is Democracy Possible?* Cambridge: Polity.

Cole, G. D. H. (1920) *Guild Socialism Re-Stated*, London: Leonard Parsons.

Cole, G. D. H. (1920) *The Social Theory*, London: Methuen.

Cole, G. D. H. (1953–61) *A History of Socialist Thought*, 5 vols, London: Macmillan.

Cristi, F. R. (1984) 'Hayek and Schmitt on the Rule of Law', *Canadian Journal of Political Science*, vol. xvii no. 3, 321–5.

Crosland, C. A. R. (1956) *The Future of Socialism*, abridged and revised edition (1964), London: Jonathan Cape.

Cutler, Tony, Karel Williams and John Williams (1986) *Keynes, Beveridge and Beyond*, London: Routledge.

Dahl, R. A. (1956) *A Preface to Democratic Theory*, Chicago: University of Chicago Press.

Dahl, R. A. (1961) *Who Governs?* New Haven: Yale University Press.

Dahl, R. A. (1970) *After the Revolution?* New Haven: Yale University Press.

Dahl, R. A. (1971) *Polyarchy*, New Haven: Yale University Press.

Dahl, R. A. (1982) *Dilemmas of Pluralist Democracies*, New Haven: Yale University Press.

Dahl, R. A. (1985) *A Preface to Economic Democracy*, Cambridge: Polity.

Duguit, Léon (1921) *Law in the Modern State*, intro. H. J. Laski, London: George Allen & Unwin. (A translation of *Transformation du droit public*, Paris, 1913.)

Durkheim, Émile (1957) *Professional Ethics and Civic Morals*, London: Routledge & Kegan Paul.

Durkheim, Émile (1962) *Socialism and Saint-Simon*, New York: Collier.

Erjin, Chen (1984) *China, Crossroads Socialism*, London: Verso.

ESECS (Europe Security Study) (1983) *Strengthening Conventional Deterrence in Europe*, London: Macmillan.

Figgis, J. N. (1913) *Churches in the Modern State*, London: Longmans.

Fitzpatrick, Peter and Alan Hunt (eds) (1987) *Critical Legal Studies*, Oxford: Basil Blackwell.

Frankel, Boris (1988) *The Post-Industrial Utopians*, Cambridge: Polity.

Freedman, L. (1981) *The Evolution of Nuclear Strategy*, London: Macmillan.

Gallie, W. B. (1978) *Philosophers of Peace and War*, Cambridge: Cambridge University Press.

Gierke, Otto von (1900) *Political Theories of the Middle Age*, intro. F. W. Maitland, Cambridge: Cambridge University Press.

Glass, S. T. (1966) *The Responsible Society*, London: Longmans.

Gorz, Andre (1982) *Farewell to the Working Class*, London: Pluto.

Habermas, Jürgen (1986) 'Sovereignty and the Fuhrerdemokratie', *Times Literary Supplement*, 26 September.

Hall, S. and D. Held (1989) 'Left and Rights', *Marxism Today*, June.

Hart, H. L. A. (1961) *The Concept of Law*, Oxford: Oxford University Press.

Hayward, J. E. S. (1960) 'Solidarist Syndicalism: Durkheim and Duguit', *Sociological Review*, vol. 8 (NS), pt. i, July, 17–36 and pt. ii Dec., 185–202.

Hegel, G. W. F. (1967) *Philosophy of Right*, trans. T. M. Knox, London: Oxford University Press.

Hindess, Barry (1982) 'Power, Interests and the Outcomes of Struggles', *Sociology*, vol. 16 no. 4.

Hindess, Barry (1984) 'Rational Choice Theory and the Analysis of Political Action', *Economy & Society*, vol. 13 no. 3, 255–75.

Hindess, Barry (ed.) (1990) *Reactions to the Right*, London: Routledge.

Hinsley, F. H. (1967) *Power and the Pursuit of Peace*, Cambridge: Cambridge University Press.

Hirst, Paul (1975) *Durkheim, Bernard and Epistemology*, London: Routledge & Kegan Paul.

Hirst, Paul (1986) *Law, Socialism and Democracy*, London: Allen & Unwin.

Hirst, Paul (1989) *After Thatcher?* London: Collins.

Hirst, Paul (ed.) (1989) *The Pluralist Theory of the State*, London: Routledge & Kegan Paul.

Hirst, Paul and Jonathan Zeitlin (eds) (1988) *Reversing Industrial Decline?* Oxford: Berg.

Howard, Michael (1981) *War and the Liberal Conscience*, Oxford: Oxford University Press.

Howard, Michael (1983) *The Causes of Wars*, London: Unwin Paperbacks.

Hsiao, K. C. (1927) *Political Pluralism*, London: Kegan Paul, Trench, Tubner & Co.

Irving, Helen (1986) 'Romanticism and British Socialism: Art and Work in Socialist Thought 1889–1920', PhD University of Sydney.

Irving, Helen (1986) 'Guilds, Corporations and Socialist Theory', *Economy and Society*, vol. 15 no. 1, 123–44.

Kant, Immanuel (1795) *On Perpetual Peace*, in *Kant on History*, trans. L. W. Beck (1963), Indianapolis, NY: Bobbs Merrill. See also *Perpetual Peace* in *Kant's Political Writings*, (ed.) H. S. Reiss, Cambridge: Cambridge University Press, 1977.

Katzenstein, Peter J. (1985) *Small States in World Markets*, Ithaca: Cornell University Press.

Kautsky, Karl (1964) *The Dictatorship of the Proletariat*, University of Michigan Press: Ann Arbor.

Keane, John (1988) *Democracy and Civil Society*, London: Verso.

Kelman, Mark (1987) *A Guide to Critical Legal Studies*, Cambridge, Mass.: Harvard University Press.

Kennedy, Ellen (1987) 'Carl Schmitt and the Frankfurt School', *Telos*, no. 71, Spring.

Kirchheimer, Otto (1969) *Politics, Law and Social Change*, ed. F. S. Burin and K. L. Shell, New York: Columbia University Press.

Kosselleck, Reinhard (1988) *Critique and Crisis*, Oxford: Berg.

Laski, H. J. (1919) *Authority in the Modern State*, New Haven, Conn.: Yale University Press.

Laski, H. J. (1921) *The Foundations of Sovereignty and Other Essays*, London: Allen & Unwin.

Lewin, Moshe (1968) *Russian Peasants and Soviet Power* London: Allen & Unwin.

Lewis, J. D. (1935) *The Genossenschaft Theory of Otto von Gierke*, Madison: University of Wisconsin Press.

Lukes, Steven (1974) *Power, A Radical View*, London: Macmillan.

Luttwak, Edward N. (1987) *Strategy: The Logic of War and Peace*, Cambridge, Mass.: The Belknap Press.

Luxemburg, Rosa (1961) *The Russian Revolution and Leninism or Marxism?* University of Michigan Press: Ann Arbor.

Marx, Karl (1871) *The Civil War in France*, in K. Marx and F. Engels, *Selected Works* (1962), vol. 1, Moscow: Foreign Language Publishing House.

McNeill, W. (1983) *The Pursuit of Power*, Oxford: Basil Blackwell.

Medvedev, Roy (1972) *Let History Judge*, London: Macmillan.

Miliband, Ralph (1969) *The State in Capitalist Society*, London: Weidenfeld & Nicholson.

Mills, C. Wright (1956) *The Power Elite*, New York: Oxford University Press.

Mouffe, Chantal (1988) 'The Civics Lesson', *New Statesman and Society*, 7 October.

Neuberg, A. (1970) *Armed Insurrection*, London: New Left Books.

Neumann, Franz (1942) *Behemoth* (1966), New York: Harper & Row.

Neumann, Franz (1957) *The Democratic and the Authoritarian State*, New York: The Free Press.

Neumann, Franz (1986) *The Rule of Law*, Leamington Spa: Berg.

Neyer, J. (1960) 'Individualism and Socialism in Durkheim', in K. H. Wolff (ed.), *Émile Durkheim, Essays on Sociology and Philosophy*, New York: Harper & Row, pp. 32–76.

Nicholls, D. (1975) *The Pluralist State*, London: Macmillan.

Ono, Shin'ya (1965) 'The Limits of Bourgeois Pluralism', *Studies on the Left*, vol. v, 46–72.

Outhwaite, William and Michael Mulkay (eds) (1987) *Social Theory and Social Criticism*, Oxford: Basil Blackwell.

Pateman, Carole (1970) *Participation and Democratic Theory*, Cambridge: Cambridge University Press.

Pearce, Frank (1989) *Radical Durkheim*, London: Unwin Hyman.

Polan, Tony (1984) *Lenin and the End of Politics*, London: Methuen.

Poulantzas, Nicos (1969) 'The Problem of the Capitalist State', *New Left Review*, no. 58, 67–78.

Poulantzas, Nicos (1973) *Political Power and Social Classes*, London: New Left Books.

Rauschning, Herman (1939) *Germany's Revolution of Destruction* (trans. of *Die Revolution des Nihilismus*), London: Heinemann.

Richter, M. (1960) 'Durkheim's Politics and Political Theory', in K. H. Wolff (ed.), *Émile Durkheim, Essays on Sociology and Philosophy*, New York: Harper & Row, pp. 170–210.

Rousseau, Jean-Jacques (1762) *The Social Contract*, trans. & intro. G. D. H. Cole (1913), London: J. M. Dent, Everyman Edn.

Schell, Jonathan (1982) *The Fate of the Earth*, London: Picador.

Schell, Jonathan (1984) *The Abolition*, London: Picador.

Schmitt, Carl (1930) 'Staatsethik und pluralistischer Staat', *Positionen und Begriffe im Kampf mit Weimar-Genf-Versailles* (1939), Hamburg: Hanseatische Verlag.

Schmitt, Carl (1932) *Legalitat und Legitimitat*, Berlin: Dunker & Humblot.

Schmitt, Carl (1976) *The Concept of the Political*, intro. G. Schwab, New Brunswick NJ: Rutgers University Press.

Schmitt, Carl (1985) *The Crisis of Parliamentary Democracy*, intro. E. Kennedy, Cambridge, Mass.: MIT Press.

Schmitt, Carl (1985) *Political Theology*, intro. G. Schwab, Cambridge, Mass.: MIT Press.

Schmitt, Carl (1986) *Political Romanticism*, trans. and intro. Guy Oakes, Cambridge, Mass.: MIT Press.

Schwab, George (1970) *The Challenge of the Exception: An Introduction to the Political Ideas of Carl Schmitt between 1921 and 1936*, Berlin: Duncker and Humblot.

Shanin, Teodor (1972) *The Awkward Class*, Oxford: Clarendon Press.

Smith, Keith (1984) *The British Economic Crisis*, Penguin: Harmondsworth.

Stone, Julius (1973) 'Two Theories of the Institution', in R. A. Newman (ed.), *Essays in Honour of Roscoe Pound*, Westport, Conn.: Greenwood Press, pp. 296–338.

Therborn, Göran (1982) 'What Does the Ruling Class Do when it Rules?' in

A. Giddens and D. Held (eds) *Classes, Power and Conflict*, London: Macmillan, pp. 224–48.

Tocqueville, Alexis de (1835) *Democracy in America* (1946), London: Oxford University Press.

Tribe, Keith (ed.) (1988) *Social Democracy and the Rule of Law*, London: Allen & Unwin.

Ulmen, G. L. (1986) 'The Sociology of the State: Carl Schmitt and Max Weber', *State, Culture and Society*, vol. 1 no. 2, Winter, 3–57.

Vincent, Steven (1984) *Pierre-Joseph Proudhon and the Origins of French Republican Socialism*, Oxford: Oxford University Press.

Weber, Max (1969) *Economy and Society*, 3 vols, New York: Bedminster Press.

Williams, Howard (1983) *Kant's Political Philosophy*, Oxford: Basil Blackwell.

Williams, Karel, John Williams and Dennis Thomas (1983) *Why are the British Bad at Manufacturing?* London: Routledge.

Wolin, Sheldon (1961) *Politics and Vision*, London: Allen & Unwin.

Wright, A. W. (1979) *G. D. H. Cole and Socialist Democracy*, Oxford: Clarendon Press.

Wright, A. W. (1986) *Socialisms*, Oxford: Oxford University Press.

Name index

Subject index